BEKAH JANE
POGUE

Praying
Your Way
to
Forgiveness

A Devotional
Prayer Journal

BARBOUR
PUBLISHING

Published by Barbour Books, an imprint of Barbour Publishing, Inc., 1810 Barbour Drive, Uhrichsville, Ohio 44683, www.barbourbooks.com

Our mission is to inspire the world with the life-changing message of the Bible.

Member of the
Evangelical Christian
Publishers Association

Printed in China.

The Great Forgiver

God, I begin this forgiveness journey focused not on who *I* need to forgive, but in gratitude for Your gracious forgiveness of *my* human side. Thank You for Your grace gift of Jesus, for Your creativity in sending One who understands human pain and relationships and weakness and covers me with His sacrifice of self. You are the Great Forgiver. In this space of humble surrender, I move forward into a life overflowing with forgiveness so that I can forgive.

Please cover me with Your strength as I explore what it looks like to assume a posture of humility and to have a soul moldable to Your Spirit. I come with an expectant heart.

Speak to me. Your humble servant is listening.

Therefore, if anyone is in Christ, the new creation has come:
The old has gone, the new is here!
2 Corinthians 5:17 niv

5

Life-Breathing Thoughts

God, as I listen to the negative self-chatter filling my mind, I realize these lies are not of You. These critical expectations and shame-filled words are taking up space where You long to breathe unconditional love and gentle words. Do You see the ways I'm so hard on myself? The stories I make up and the shame I readily dump on my good intents? I'd never speak to my kids or friends this way, and therefore, I want to be gracious with myself as well.

Forgive me, Father. Please replace self-loathing thoughts with thoughts that are beautiful and true and saturated in self-control, thoughts that breathe life and declutter the lies. Spirit, please redirect my negative self-talk with whatever is pure and lovely and true so that I may go about my day open to Your truths and with space to receive.

Finally, brothers and sisters, whatever is true, whatever is noble, whatever is right, whatever is pure, whatever is lovely, whatever is admirable— if anything is excellent or praiseworthy—think about such things. Whatever you have learned or received or heard from me, or seen in me—put it into practice. And the God of peace will be with you.
PHILIPPIANS 4:8–9 NIV

My Hope

God, today I'm soul weary and in need of hope. I confess I feel anxious about my current circumstances and desperately need You to fill me from the inside out. When I focus on what's lacking, I feel heavy inside, and as much as I don't want to feel this way, I do.

Thank You for loving me just as I am. Forgive me for focusing on my circumstances, which shift like the weather. Invite me to cling to You; my steadfast, unwavering hope is found in You alone. Whether in plenty or want, my heart desperately wants You to lighten the weight inside and fill me with expectancy of Your spirit. Where anxiety threatens, I'm asking for You to stir me to pray aloud, *God, be my hope.*

Let us hold unswervingly to the hope we profess, for he who promised is faithful.
Hebrews 10:23 niv

A Confession of Pride

Ha! God, today I became aware of my pride when I found myself comparing and coming out ahead: *Look how helpful I am. Man, my family and friends are so lucky to have me in their life. Where would they be without me? I nailed it today at helping and serving.*

Gulp. True confession. I acknowledge my pride and ask for Your forgiveness in elevating the gifts You gave me and believing I somehow don't need You. Turn my heart from pride and create a tender, teachable spirit in me. For without You, my gifts are self-made and given with selfish ambition. Help me live alive in who You are constantly creating me to be: a reflection of You. And remind me, even now, that You laugh with me and delight in my pure intentions, even when they emerge with pride.

Do nothing out of selfish ambition or vain conceit. Rather,
in humility value others above yourselves, not looking to your
own interests but each of you to the interests of the others.
Philippians 2:3–4 NIV

Free and Uninhibited

God, today I saw a little girl walk up to another girl at a restaurant and introduce herself. "You wanna play?" she asked innocently. I want to be that little girl again. Childlike confidence. A willingness to laugh and play and befriend perfect strangers. I admit, becoming an adult dulls the free spirit inside, and I ask for Your forgiveness for dimming the light You placed in me from birth.

Father, renew that little girl inside me. Invite me to laugh until I snort and to play hard, without care for what others think. Please quiet the lies that threaten to silence a playful spirit and childlike faith. Bring to mind ways I was most alive when I was younger, and invite me to live free and uninhibited. May I resolve to journey toward joy and leave laughter in my wake.

When the Lord restored the fortunes of Zion, we were like those who dream. Then our mouth was filled with laughter, and our tongue with shouts of joy; then they said among the nations, "The Lord has done great things for them." The Lord has done great things for us; we are glad.
PSALM 126:1–3 ESV

A Restart

Lord, today my patience well is dry. I'm frustrated with my kids, my temper is short, and I admit, I'm not momming well. In fact, I'd like to relieve myself of mom duties at the moment and crawl back into bed. Thank You for hearing me and understanding, as a parent Yourself. God, where criticalness is at an all-time high, would You replace that with compassion? Where anger comes in a raised voice, would You replace it with a gentle response? God, I need a deep breath, a restart. Would You help me to see my children's hearts with Your lens—beyond their behavior and straight into their souls? May I scoop them up and whisper sincere love and affirmations over them. And would You do the same for me, my gentle, loving Father, in the moments when I'm quick to beat myself up? After all, I am Your kid too, and sometimes I just need a heavenly hug.

A hot-tempered person stirs up conflict, but the one who is patient calms a quarrel.
Proverbs 15:18 niv

Trading Comparison for Contentment

Okay, God, I'm finding myself looking around and comparing. *They get to go on vacation. Their marriage looks perfect. I bet their kids are always respectful. Oh look, they're remodeling their kitchen.*

Jealousy.

I'm embarrassed, but this is my true heart. Would You please forgive me? God, You are taking care of me. You care about feeding birds and clothing wildflowers; help me trust that You are giving me more than I need.

Please replace my comparison with a content heart. One that is thankful and quick to give You praise for what *is* happening, what *is* my reality: a heartbeat, health, this roof above my head. Give me thankful awareness for the clothes I wear, the people that come across my path, and this life that's a gift. In You, my soul finds contentment.

"If God so clothes the grass, which is alive in the field today, and tomorrow is thrown into the oven, how much more will he clothe you, O you of little faith! . . . All the nations of the world seek after these things, and your Father knows that you need them. Instead, seek his kingdom, and these things will be added to you."
Luke 12:28, 30–31 ESV

A Prayer for a Hurting Heart

God, my heart is hurt. There are people I feel unseen and misunderstood by. Legitimate, real hurts, and I can't flip a switch and suddenly forgive. Please assure me that You see my hurting heart and understand my pain. You appreciate my honesty and don't want me to cover up my true feelings. Even in my inability to forgive, please make my heart a little more tender and moldable than yesterday.

Can You please remind me how You see me today so that I can claim Your promises and take one small step toward ultimate forgiveness? Thank You for Your patience with my process. I trust You are making all things beautiful in Your time. Soften my heart even as I work and walk and tune my ear to Your Word.

He has made everything beautiful in its time.
Also, he has put eternity into man's heart, yet so that he cannot
find out what God has done from the beginning to the end.
ECCLESIASTES 3:11 ESV

Thanks in the Everyday-ness

God, I admit, as I'm washing dishes, that I forget to thank You for the everyday provisions like plates and forks and food. How much I have to be thankful for and how often I neglect to pause and thank You first for the miraculously minuscule ways You show up—in weekday dinners and dirty silverware. These reminders are Your invitation for community, eating with neighbors, and enjoying recipes together. The dish washing is the celebration for a meal well spent, conversations well shared. Plates and forks joyfully messed. Forgive me for complaining instead of rejoicing. Turn my heart now toward praise. Yay for dirty dishes, for each one signifies a person fed nourishment and soul care in my home. May You be the center of every meal and conversation from this day forward.

Whatever you do, work at it with all your heart, as working for the Lord, not for human masters, since you know that you will receive an inheritance from the Lord as a reward. It is the Lord Christ you are serving.
Colossians 3:23–24 niv

Help Me to Notice

God, as I dig my hands in the dirt and press my face near the damp soil, I am thankful to plant life into the ground. I am stilled with awe at how You spoke the world into existence. Such creativity. Such wonder. Who would've thought to make giraffes and gardenias? Mud and squirmy worms? Help me pause with knees bent and hands in the dirt as an act of worship. Help me notice today as a canvas of Your creativity. As I plant these seeds, tether my heart to their growth and connect my intimacy to You. In the same way, please shine Your face upon mine. May I reflect You in word and action.

From this place, God, I long to grow more like You and less in my own image. May I bear a harvest of joy, hope, and grace, and abide in Your steadfast love.

For as the soil makes the sprout come up and a garden causes seeds to grow, so the Sovereign LORD will make righteousness and praise spring up before all nations.
ISAIAH 61:11 NIV

Kingdom Perspective

God, You say the kingdom is like a mustard seed, and mustard seeds are small. How often do I think of the word *kingdom* and imagine big, flashy, and powerful? To You, kingdom perspective is about the heart. Forgive me for getting caught up in the world's perspective of kingdom instead of Your eternal kingdom. Stir me toward grand in Your eyes—small as a mustard seed. This is my goal.

Whisper Your delight in me as I go about the small tasks of my day. Please remind me that these mustard seed miracles are building "the largest of plants" where shade and refuge will be available to others. I desire to have a heart that follows Your lead, regardless of outcome or status. Your kingdom is coming, and what matters most is my eternal deposits I'm making on earth: You and people. This is enough.

He told them another parable: "The kingdom of heaven is like a mustard seed, which a man took and planted in his field. Though it is the smallest of all seeds, yet when it grows, it is the largest of garden plants and becomes a tree, so that the birds come and perch in its branches."
MATTHEW 13:31–32 NIV

A Rhythm of Dependence

Like the familiar hymn, Lord, *I need You, oh, I need You, every hour I need You.*

God, I desperately want to depend on You and acknowledge how much easier it is for me to kick into self-dependence. Forgive me for relying on myself, my strength, my pep-talk spirit. I confess I am weary and don't want to go another minute on my own. Help me, even as I struggle to understand what it means to fully depend on You. Help me pay attention when I release control, and when I greedily take charge.

Awaken me to what dependence looks like with You, so that I may create a rhythm of laying myself aside in order that You may lead. And as I do, God, please help me feel lighter inside, in ways only Your Spirit can. This is my heart's cry.

The heart of man plans his way, but the LORD establishes his steps.
PROVERBS 16:9 ESV

The Sheer Beauty of Creating

I am made in the image of the mighty Creator and therefore am creative. God, awaken me to ways that You made me to feel alive while creating. Is it picking wildflowers and pressing them between book pages to make art? Is it baking cookies for the neighborhood kids? Is it singing? Writing? Quilting? Whatever the creative magic You sewed into me since before time, pull that out of me today. Help me delight in creating for the sheer beauty of creating—not the final result, but the joy in the creative process. Forgive me when I forget that this spark You've given me is unique; no one else has the same way of creating from my perspective. Help me not squander but generously use my gift. I'm so thankful I have a Father who enjoys making and creating and living alive in this creative space.

"He has filled them with skill to do all kinds of work as engravers, designers, embroiderers in blue, purple and scarlet yarn and fine linen, and weavers—all of them skilled workers and designers."
Exodus 35:35 niv

Patient Perseverance

God, I'm laughing because You know me and my urgency to move quickly, to activate, to check off boxes and focus on the next task. Still me, Lord. Please shift my activator mind-set toward patient perseverance—slow and steady. A steadfast tenacity to keep going despite difficulty in seeing success or an outcome. This is faith. This is trust.

Rest my soul. I breathe deep of Your love. Your time frame is contingent, not on success, but on matters of the soul. You are not worried about my achievements but care mostly about equipping me with strength for the journey. Patient perseverance is my prayer. I ask confidently and know You are restoring my steps for today.

The LORD is my shepherd; I shall not want. He makes me lie down in green pastures. He leads me beside still waters. He restores my soul. He leads me in paths of righteousness for his name's sake.
PSALM 23:1–3 ESV

Longing for Intimacy and Wholeness

God, marriage is hard. I sometimes find myself leading with criticism instead of compassion. I'm so sorry. I know You see my heart—my longing for intimacy and wholeness with my spouse. I need encouragement to stay on the path You have for me—to take responsibility for my words, thoughts, and actions. Help me care for my spouse without feeling like I need to carry him. Help me untangle any resentment or unspoken anger I'm harboring. Please help me own my issues without pointing fingers or waiting for him to change before I step into healing and forgiveness.

Soften my heart, God. Please restore compassion where criticalness is present. Reignite my love for him. Strengthen me, for I am weak. Help me walk under the cloak of Your strength and know Your intimacy so that I may love from an overflow.

"My grace is sufficient for you, for my power is made perfect in weakness." Therefore I will boast all the more gladly about my weaknesses, so that Christ's power may rest on me. That is why, for Christ's sake, I delight in weaknesses, in insults, in hardships, in persecutions, in difficulties. For when I am weak, then I am strong.
2 Corinthians 12:9–10 niv

Baking Therapy

Lord, baking is my therapy. Something about cracking eggs and stirring flour calms my soul. I put on music and lose myself to the joy of baking. I imagine You sitting in the kitchen with me, while I get out bowls and dance while mixing ingredients. God, I want this type of real-time relationship with You. A relationship of friendship. Of talking about our day, and baking, and being in each other's presence. A relationship of laughter and fun and ease. Help me notice You in these everyday ways. And may what I'm baking be a sacrifice of time—not only to the people I feed—but to You.

You fed the Israelites morning manna for their journey. Jesus, You multiplied loaves of bread for the masses. My sacrifice is this baked good. May it be pleasing to You and a symbol of my repentant spirit for the ultimate sacrifice of Your Son, my Savior.

"You shall take fine flour and bake twelve loaves from it; two tenths of an ephah shall be in each loaf. And you shall set them in two piles, six in a pile, on the table of pure gold before the LORD."
LEVITICUS 24:5–6 ESV

Active Listening

God, help me listen to Your voice more than anyone else's. With all the voices and noise and buzz on social media, in our communities, and even in my home, I can easily forget pausing, being still, and actively listening to You.

God, I'm sorry for being quick to offer my ears to what is urgent and reactive, rather than responsive and slow. Your words come in the quiet, in the everyday, and I long to still myself to listen—really listen—and then actively respond and step obediently into where You are calling me. Forgive me for listening to others first. For creating idols in well-intentioned relationships before filtering my heart with You first.

I quiet myself before You. I'm here. Expectantly listening to Your voice.

"These things I have spoken to you while I am still with you. But the Helper, the Holy Spirit, whom the Father will send in my name, he will teach you all things and bring to your remembrance all that I have said to you."
JOHN 14:25–26 ESV

Self-Care

God, I need permission. Permission to not have the answers or be all the things for all the people. Permission to simply be. Permission to take care of myself. The world sees this as selfish, but God, I know You say caring for my soul is healthy and good. I am no good if I'm not first tending to my soul and body. Would You whisper respite and rest over me?

Forgive me for running too fast to the detriment of my body and heart. What does my soul need, Father? Is it a walk? My favorite coffee? Curling up with a good book? Is it a night out with a friend and laughing until I cry? Stir in me what it is I need, and be my permission today.

But I speak this by permission, and not of commandment. For I would
that all men were even as I myself. But every man hath his proper
gift of God, one after this manner, and another after that.
1 Corinthians 7:6–7 kjv

Delightful Celebration

God, I find it easy to celebrate when life is going as planned, when circumstances are favorable and comfortable. Yet, I know You do Your greatest work in my discomfort. But for today, I will rejoice. I will tuck this moment away and pull it out for the hard days.

As Job said, we are so quick to praise in the good and complain in the hard. Forgive me, God, for treating You like a genie and questioning Your ways when life goes off course. Today, I will pull out the fancy china, sing in the car, and smile at every stranger. I will celebrate, for I am savoring every moment, every feeling, every creation sighting and conversation. You are in all of this, and to You I give thanks and experience sheer and utter delight!

Rejoice in the Lord always. I will say it again: Rejoice! Let your gentleness be evident to all. The Lord is near. Do not be anxious about anything, but in every situation, by prayer and petition, with thanksgiving, present your requests to God. And the peace of God, which transcends all understanding, will guard your hearts and your minds in Christ Jesus.
PHILIPPIANS 4:4–7 NIV

The Beauty of a Sunset

God, I'm sitting on the porch, watching the sunset, and I'm in absolute awe of Your gifts of color—the way the apricot hues merge with stormy violets and the sunshine creates cloud outlines in the sky. How I love watching the sun set! As I do, I'm reminded that it's the close of the day.

How did I hear You today? Where did I see You? How were You wooing me to Your Spirit? What sounds and sights did You use to speak directly to my soul? What colors invited me to pause and take notice?

Who am I that You are aware and mindful of me? Yet, I'm so thankful You are. As I rock on this porch, I'm enraptured with Your creative beauty. I'm closing my eyes and saving this moment in my memory bank—a sky painting delivered from my heavenly Father, a one-of-a-kind piece of art.

The whole earth is filled with awe at your wonders; where morning dawns, where evening fades, you call forth songs of joy.
PSALM 65:8 NIV

Provision

God, I confess: I'm freaking out about finances. The bills are piling up and work is slow, and I find myself waking with my heart pounding from worry.

I don't understand why finances feel so heavy. Help me cling to the truth that You are my Provider. Help me surrender my desire to control or kick into hustling, and instead, trust.

Maybe provision doesn't come in dollar bills but through the generosity of neighbors. Through understanding what others experience when they are struggling financially. Please use this struggle to grow my compassion and to offer a safe space for others to confess their financial struggles as well. Help me see Your out-of-the-box provisions that I would miss if I didn't need You like I do. Please root in me a reminder that whether I am in plenty or want, I am content in You.

I know what it is to be in need, and I know what it is to have plenty.
I have learned the secret of being content in any and every situation,
whether well fed or hungry, whether living in plenty or in want.
I can do all this through him who gives me strength.
PHILIPPIANS 4:12–13 NIV

A Deep Breath of Grace

God, I'm noticing that my grace well is dry. I'm cranky and selfish, and life seems half empty. Thank You for loving me as I am, but I know You desire more; You long for me to believe You saved me by Your grace, and because of this, I can fully offer grace to those around me. Offer me a deep breath of grace right now. I don't have to work for Your love—I'm covered. May this knowledge sink into my bones.

God, I want to be a soul who lavishes grace because I know of my need for Your grace first. Soak my soul in the gift of knowing You. As I spend time with You, may grace naturally overflow. A grace giver is who I want to be. Forgive me for expecting this gift when I'm quick to expect others to earn their favor from me. Grace upon grace upon grace is my prayer.

For by grace you have been saved through faith.
And this is not your own doing; it is the gift of God,
not a result of works, so that no one may boast.
Ephesians 2:8–9 esv

Welcoming Well

God, sometimes I'm insecure and hold back from flinging my door open and inviting people over. Who cares if my home is lived in and imperfectly messy? Forgive me for waiting until it's clean and clothes are put away and I'm nice and tidy before practicing hospitality. Forgive me for caring too much about doing it *right*, rather than welcoming well. Please help me look past clean counters to those who need a safe space to connect, to be heard, to sit on my couch and be fully known and fully loved.

Nudge me to invite those who come to mind. Hospitality is lavish welcoming, and I can do this through encouragement or a phone call, or by baking cookies and having an impromptu dessert night. God, it's my heart You want, and may this home be a conduit of Your love and healing for all who enter and for however long they stay. The dirty dishes can wait!

Above all, love each other deeply, because love covers over a multitude of sins. Offer hospitality to one another without grumbling. Each of you should use whatever gift you have received to serve others, as faithful stewards of God's grace in its various forms.
1 Peter 4:8–10 niv

True Comfort Restoration

God, I hate being uncomfortable. I want to squirm free, push past this tension, and move onto the next comfortable thing.

I know staying in this space helps me depend on You for true comfort. Help me listen to my body and pay attention to when I'm uncomfortable and how I respond. How do I rush to squelch my anxiety? How are You inviting me to stay in this discomfort and why?

God, I acknowledge that when I'm uncomfortable, the ugliest parts come to the surface. As they do, would You please comfort me in my discomfort? Tether me close to Your Spirit so that when I'm anxious and scared and frantic to move from this space, I'll sense You drawing me to stay here and know what true comfort restoration looks like.

Your hands made me and formed me; give me understanding to learn
your commands. May those who fear you rejoice when they see me,
for I have put my hope in your word. I know, LORD, that your laws are
righteous, and that in faithfulness you have afflicted me. May your
unfailing love be my comfort, according to your promise to your servant.
PSALM 119:73–76 NIV

Truth-Telling

God, there are secrets and thoughts I don't feel like I can talk about with anyone. What will they say? Will they judge me?

Here's the thing: I want to tell my truth and feel confident in sharing my heart and experience. Even if no one understands, I know I'll feel better for getting these bouncing-around thoughts out into the open air. Healing awaits in truth-telling, and hopefully by sharing my heart, I can encourage others and open a safe space for my friends and family to share their truths.

God, forgive me for hiding in shame and letting fear overpower my courage to share honestly. Who are safe people I can share with? Please bring those people to mind and stir me to share boldly. I'm asking for Your strength to continue sharing my truths and finding my identity and worth in Your truth and Your words.

O LORD, who shall sojourn in your tent? Who shall dwell on your holy hill? He who walks blamelessly and does what is right and speaks truth in his heart; who does not slander with his tongue and does no evil to his neighbor, nor takes up a reproach against his friend.
PSALM 15:1–3 ESV

More Than What Is Seen

God, forgive me for expecting others to think and respond like I do. How are they to crawl inside my mind and know what's going on in there? How am I to understand what anyone is going through without living their life?

There is always more than what is seen. Hidden hurts. Huge dreams. Quiet confessions. I need Your lens to see people the way You do. To allow them to learn at their speed, to experience You in their unique ways, to be who You created them to be. I know I need people to extend grace for my journey, and I want Your understanding to offer that to others.

Where I'm quick to be impatient, would You please tender my heart toward learning? Where I am quick to make assumptions or have uncommunicated expectations, would You help me pause and listen to their story without judgment? God, make me inclusive, just as You are.

Whoever is patient has great understanding,
but one who is quick-tempered displays folly.
PROVERBS 14:29 NIV

30

A Broken Heart for the Brokenhearted

God, my heart is so sad for my friend who lost a loved one. I want to get in my car and drive to see her and hug her neck and tell her I'm so sorry about her loss. I admit, I don't know what to say. I don't know how she feels. What I do know is that You relate to our suffering. You know grief and sadness, and Your heart breaks when ours does. Forgive me for wanting to rescue her from her grief.

What does she need, Lord? How can I be there in her pain? Does she simply need a safe space to be sad?

Thank You for bringing me near the brokenhearted so that I can better understand how You felt when Your heart was breaking. Break my heart for those that are broken so I may know Your nearness with them.

The righteous cry out, and the Lord hears them; he delivers them from all their troubles. The Lord is close to the brokenhearted and saves those who are crushed in spirit.
Psalm 34:17–18 niv

Flashes of Anger

God, I'm angry. I feel that hot flash of electricity course through me. I feel embarrassed by my strong emotions, but they are honest.

What is simmering beneath my anger? Hurt? Sadness? How can I allow myself to process my anger in a healthy way so that, ultimately, I can heal? I'm offering this anger to You, God. I know You aren't asking me to cover it up or shove it down deep, but to bring it out into the open and let Your Spirit slowly heal my anger.

Thank You for offering space for me to come as I am, anger and all. You don't tell me I'm too much or to get over it. You know anger. You've been there. How are You inviting me not to sin in my anger and using this emotion to lead me toward righteousness in You? Do Your deep work in me, Lord. Please heal me from the inside out.

"In your anger do not sin": Do not let the sun go down while
you are still angry, and do not give the devil a foothold.
Ephesians 4:26–27 niv

32

Empathy and Connection

God, today I walked past a homeless woman and, I'll admit, felt quick judgment. What did she do to get here? Is she on drugs? What's her story?

Forgive me, Lord, for being fast to think I'm better because I have a home to sleep in. The only thing separating me from her is circumstance. Forgive me for elevating myself at another's expense. Didn't You lead by joining the outcast, the homeless, the less-than? Aren't these the very people You ate with and loved well? My heart breaks at how judgmental I am. Moving forward, please shift me toward empathy and connection with those who sleep on sidewalks and in homes alike.

"Is not this the fast that I choose. . . ? Is it not to share your bread with the hungry and bring the homeless poor into your house; when you see the naked, to cover him, and not to hide yourself from your own flesh? Then shall your light break forth like the dawn, and your healing shall spring up speedily; your righteousness shall go before you; the glory of the LORD shall be your rear guard."
ISAIAH 58:6–8 ESV

Gift of Health

My body aches, and I feel miserable. I don't have time to be sick. I'm humbled, God, because it's in my sickness that I am ever so aware of the many days I'm healthy. How quick I am to complain when I'm in bed but forget to praise You for the days I wake healthy and strong. I repent of this everyday miracle of health.

Health is a daily gift. Forgive me for taking this for granted. Today I will rest. I put on music and rest my body in soft sheets and pretend You are holding me while I'm ill. Use this ailment to deepen my dependency and humble me more to Your Spirit. Awaken me to ways that the world goes on while I lie here resting. Invite me to further surrender my control and receive rest from You.

This was to fulfill what was spoken through the prophet Isaiah:
"He took up our infirmities and bore our diseases."
MATTHEW 8:17 NIV

Beauty All Around

God, I look outside and see the vibrant green of grass and yellow flashes of wildflowers. Your beauty is everywhere, waiting to be enjoyed. Every delicate flower, the blue of the sky, the way the clouds form shapes and wisp across the horizon. . . Draw me to notice Your beauty in every person I interact with, the cup I drink from, and the architecture of buildings.

You waste nothing in design and structure and nature. Even when I cut an apple horizontally, there is Your beauty staring back in the form of a star. I'm aware of how often I take Your beauty for granted, for all of this—the beach, culture, various dialects, people, forests, and waves—is merely a facet of Your beauty.

God, how I want the earth's beauty to be an overarching imitation of the beauty You are. How I long to be in Your presence one day and behold Your infinite beauty.

"Consider how the wild flowers grow. They do not labor or spin. Yet I tell you, not even Solomon in all his splendor was dressed like one of these."
LUKE 12:27 NIV

The Blame Game

God, here's my honest confession: I want to blame others for my situation. I want to blame my husband for his impatient words. I want to blame my kids for arguing. I want to blame the mailman for not bringing my magazine on time. I want to blame our finances for not being larger. Blame, blame, blame.

Forgive me, Lord. Please turn my heart to notice where I need to take responsibility.

What is at the root of my blaming? What is my truth? What are my choices today? Help me walk confidently on the path You have for me without looking at others or beginning sentences with other people's names. Lord, I know You long to shift my blaming habit toward responsibility and bring freedom. There is power in owning my choices, and today I start this new habit. Thank You!

For each will have to bear his own load. Let the one who is taught the word share all good things with the one who teaches.
GALATIANS 6:5–6 ESV

Protective Mom Syndrome

God, my sweet boy woke last night with anxiety. When he lay down next to me, I could feel his heart beating fast, like a jackhammer. God, how I love him and want to protect him from anxiety and bad dreams. You are a parent; You understand this desire to shield a child from fear.

In his anxiety, help me listen instead of trying to fix him. I need Your wisdom for the words to speak and how to pray over him. May I be in tune with You so closely that I'm simply a conduit of Your voice as I whisper over his restless body.

Cover him with Your peace. Help me be a place of safety for him to bring his fear and rest in my arms. Is there specific scripture You can bring to mind that I can pray over him before he sleeps? Please use my boy's anxiety so I'll depend even more on You for wisdom on how to parent his heart.

Anxiety weighs down the heart, but a kind word cheers it up.
PROVERBS 12:25 NIV

A Glimpse of a Smile

I passed my reflection in the mirror, then a storefront window, then the car rearview mirror and noticed my smile. It was missing. In its place was a furrowed brow and focused scowl. How sad. How sad that when I catch a glimpse of my face, it's unsmiling.

God, please forgive me for being so focused on the next task that I forget to carry Your joy on my face. A smile is a free gift—a reminder that *all* of life is a gift. In the morning, Lord, will You please nudge me to first notice Your joy that fills me from the inside? Will You prompt me to dress my face with a smile—a genuine expression that reflects the deep knowledge that the Holy Spirit dwells within me? What do I have to fear? What is more important than this?

God, please continue to use my countenance to display that my soul and smile are from You.

A happy heart makes the face cheerful, but heartache crushes the spirit. The discerning heart seeks knowledge, but the mouth of a fool feeds on folly. All the days of the oppressed are wretched, but the cheerful heart has a continual feast.
PROVERBS 15:13–15 NIV

Unconditional Love

God, I'm not feeling the love. I feel misunderstood by a family member, and all I want is to be loved by her—*unconditionally*. This season leaves me weary, with little left to give. I realize my sadness at wanting to be loved by this person, when really, I first need that unconditional love from You.

Lord, You know my heart. Please offer wisdom to know what unconditional love is as I draw from You as the Source and experience Your vast, endless, east-is-to-the-west love and forgiveness.

May Your love be my compass to offer love to others. Please help me discern what is and isn't love in return. Help me be strong in maintaining healthy expectations and boundaries, even while I crave love from this person. Please fill me with Your endless love, Lord.

"The Lord appeared to him from far away. I have loved
you with an everlasting love; therefore I have
continued my faithfulness to you."
Jeremiah 31:3 esv

Strength in Weakness

God, please forgive me. I am heaping shame on myself for not being tougher, for being too emotional. This is not of You. You made me with emotions. You don't expect me to stuff them down or pep talk them away.

Please use my weakness, the areas I feel most dependent and needy, to find my need in You. Forgive me for trying to be tough and positive on my own. Forgive me for harsh self-talk. Please tender me with a sensitive spirit to find my strength in Your "enoughness."

God, You say that when I am weakest, Your power is the strongest. I need Your strength to fill in my weak spaces. I offer my brokenness, my weariness, my weakness, and I trust You are doing a beautiful work of renewing strength void of anything I can do on my own. Please rest Your power upon me, God. I will walk under Your strong covering just as I am, weakness and all.

But he said to me, "My grace is sufficient for you, for my power is made perfect in weakness." Therefore I will boast all the more gladly of my weaknesses, so that the power of Christ may rest upon me.
2 Corinthians 12:9 esv

Spiritual Life Mentors

Jesus, I find myself longing for an older woman to spend time with and glean wisdom from. Someone who is farther along on her spiritual life journey who will sit with me and offer perspective and truthful wisdom. I know this desire toward growth and health and learning is from You.

Would You please bring a woman in my path who would be interested in mentoring me? Also, please help me be aware of someone younger I can be a mentor to. Life is about community—about learning from one another and sharing our stories and faith experiences. Help me to be aware of who is in my path and to take every opportunity to listen and encourage individuals toward You.

Shepherd the flock of God that is among you, exercising oversight, not under compulsion, but willingly, as God would have you; not for shameful gain, but eagerly; not domineering over those in your charge, but being examples to the flock. And when the chief Shepherd appears, you will receive the unfading crown of glory.
1 Peter 5:2–4 esv

Trusting in the Tiniest Details

God, I feel funny asking this, but as I grab my library bag, would You please draw me toward what You want me to read? I believe You are in all of life, including the books I read. Draw me toward a message of hope. Stir me toward a change of heart.

Would You please draw me toward what author You want to speak through? Isn't it amazing how someone can write words that years later touch another's soul? For such a time as this, right?

Help me trust Your lead in the tiniest of details, including library trips and book reads. Please cement my eyes to what strengthens my faith and makes me think deeper and pay more attention to Your work in all of life. For what I read is what I store in my heart. May it be pleasing to You.

For the word of God is alive and active. Sharper than any double-edged sword, it penetrates even to dividing soul and spirit, joints and marrow; it judges the thoughts and attitudes of the heart.
HEBREWS 4:12 NIV

A Heart of Gratitude

God, I confess that today I want ALL THE THINGS. A new house, a new spouse, more space. If I'm being honest, I even want new kids. I want to update my decor and wardrobe and furniture, and even my friends feel old. I'm dissatisfied and embarrassed to admit my feelings. Yet I will, because if I can't be honest with You, who already knows all my thoughts, then who?

Please forgive my selfishness and turn me toward a heart of gratitude. I needn't look far to see how I already have much to be thankful for. God, if I can't be thankful with small things, how am I to be thankful when huge miracles happen? Please tender me to pay attention to the very space in which I stand, and work outward, noting every person, thing, and circumstance as an absolute gift. Instead of spending energy on what *isn't*, please help me be thankful for all You *have* given.

But godliness with contentment is great gain, for we brought nothing into the world, and we cannot take anything out of the world. But if we have food and clothing, with these we will be content.
1 Timothy 6:6–8 esv

A Change in the Weather

God, the weather is changing. And as it does, would You turn my soul with it? Toward a new way of seeing You? My neighborhood? This community? There's beauty in shifting seasons, for they invite our hearts into a fresh mind-set.

Please give me courage to lay down habits and relationships that are heavy and toxic. I'm following You and will continue stepping into this next season with an openness to how You are leading, revealing, and making all things new.

Forgive me for standing stubbornly in security and comfort. I open my hands and heart to You now, even as the temperature and weather changes. Please invite me deeper into Your heart and give me strength to release what I no longer need to grasp tightly to so that I may free myself to cling to You. Please use this change in weather to uncover a deeper awareness of You.

"While the earth remains, seedtime and harvest, cold and heat, summer and winter, day and night, shall not cease."
GENESIS 8:22 ESV

Only Love and Grace

I did it again. I lost my temper because my husband didn't read my mind. *Why do I do that? Why do I expect him to know what I'm thinking?* Lord, please forgive me for having unspoken expectations, which only lead to unmet expectations. Only You know my thoughts before I do. Please help me pay attention to what I'm feeling.

What is going on in my head? My heart? My body? What do I need? How can I best communicate my honest thoughts with my spouse? Please be with me as I'm learning to communicate, even after all these years. Thank You for Your grace. I'm asking for additional grace as I confess my expectations to my hubby and ask for his forgiveness.

Thank You for encouraging us to bring our honest hearts to one another and find grace in communicating. Mostly, please give me a sense of humor to let my spouse and myself off the hook. Shame is not welcome here. Only love and grace.

Let us then approach God's throne of grace with confidence, so that we may receive mercy and find grace to help us in our time of need.
HEBREWS 4:16 NIV

45

Trust in Protection

God, today I feel exposed and vulnerable. There are some projects I'm diving into and dreams I'm pursuing. I know You are inviting me to obediently follow, but as soon as the quiet settles, I find myself scared.

How will this go? Will it flop? Does anyone care? Will this work? I don't have answers, but even in my vulnerability I confess how quickly I want to self-protect. I want to pad myself with comfort and retreat to safety. To what is known and secure. Yet, following You means living exposed and stepping willingly into the unknown. Forgive me for wanting to stay where I'm safe and cozy rather than willingly going into the wilderness.

God, will You please cover me with Your protection when I'm tempted to self-protect? Self-protecting doesn't allow my vulnerable self to be transformed—only my outermost shell. I give You all of me. Help me trust Your protection even when I feel exposed.

The LORD is good, a stronghold in the day of trouble;
he knows those who take refuge in him.
NAHUM 1:7 ESV

Complete Space

Jesus, I interrupt and put words in a friend's mouth, and that isn't helpful. I finish her sentences and assume I know where her verbal thoughts are leading. I'm impatient with her storytelling and interject and speak for her. I'm aware of this bad habit, and I don't like this shadow side of my ego.

Why do I speak for her? Why am I impatient? How would listening serve her better?

Jesus, please forgive me for being quick to speak and slow to listen. Help me go into this conversation to enjoy and fully listen without interrupting or adding my own spin. Moreover, please offer awareness of when I do this so that I can pause and apologize to her in the moment and invite her to share without fear of being cut off.

The most beautiful gift we can offer one another is complete space to share and be heard. This is my heartbeat, and I need Your wisdom for how to listen well and completely.

Do nothing from selfish ambition or conceit, but in humility count others more significant than yourselves.
Philippians 2:3 esv

A Deep-Rooted Confidence

God, it seems the more I listen to Your voice and surrender my security, the crazier I feel. I've even had some family and friends caution me to stop asking so many questions and just have more faith. Yet, there's an inner tug to step out of what I know to step into a deeper relationship with You.

This feels scary because I'm not sure where I'm going or how the journey will unfold, but I know it's one of deep soul work. Humans look at the outward appearance, but You look at my heart. Please forgive me for pushing You aside because I get distracted by others' disapproval. God, I crave a deeper relationship with You, even if this means discomfort in my other relationships. Please root in me a confidence in Your voice and the obedience to listen and follow.

For the LORD will be your confidence
and will keep your foot from being caught.
PROVERBS 3:26 ESV

A Shift in Perspective

I read a story about a man who had nothing but a small cow that nourished his starving family. The cow was stolen in the middle of the night, and they discovered later that it had fallen from a cliff and died. The cow's death forced them to shift their perspective from what was barely working and invited them to start something new. Years later, the family flourished and went on to create businesses and build a large home and lead a robust life.

God, what is the "cow" in my life that's blocking me from seeing the potential You created in me? Where do I need to shift my perspective? How are You using circumstantial pain as a catalyst to Your greater good? Forgive me for cursing at this annoyance, and please give me patience to trust You for what is yet not seen or understood. Perhaps the death of my current dream is paving space for Your ultimate dream.

And we know that for those who love God all things work together
for good, for those who are called according to his purpose.
Romans 8:28 esv

....
....
....
....
....
....
....
....
....

49

Abiding

Jesus, I like the idea of abiding, but doing it is another matter altogether. Abiding means to endure, to stay the course and cling to You for the long haul. Lord, I confess, I want the quick answers, the blessings to abound. I want the flowers before I've done the long work of being tucked into the soil and taken long days, darkness, and time to bloom.

What is it about abiding that I'm fighting? What part is hard? Jesus, as I notice this push against staying in You, I sense that the waiting and depending causes anxiety. How long do I need to abide? When will the fruit come?

Forgive me for focusing on the fruit instead of melting into Your branches. How I long to rest in Your love and let Your work be done in Your time, so that You are the One who is glorified.

"Abide in me, and I in you. As the branch cannot bear fruit by itself, unless it abides in the vine, neither can you, unless you abide in me. I am the vine; you are the branches. Whoever abides in me and I in him, he it is that bears much fruit."
JOHN 15:4–5 ESV

Eager to Experience

God, I wake eager to experience You in the tiny details of today. Before I get out of bed, would You please clear my mind of clutter and distractions so that I can approach the day open and ready to listen. As I go about work, cleaning, everyday tasks, would You help me notice how Your Spirit meets me in my senses?

Where am I hearing You? What are You saying? What smells evoke memories of when I'm most alive? What tangible things do I touch that turn a grateful heart to You? What am I reading, and is it truth-honoring? Are the foods I eat out of coping or nourishment?

Please help me notice the personal ways You woo me and meet me right where I am: at the grocery store, talking with a coworker, and preparing dinner. I often neglect to say yes to Your all-sensory invitations knocking at every turn. Still my heart to notice, and may I answer with anticipation and a gladness of spirit.

"For the ear tests words as the palate tastes food."
JOB 34:3 ESV

Self-Control

God, I'm sorry. I acknowledge that I need self-control. I'm prone to react and impatiently tap my foot and yell when I'm not getting my way. I'm like a toddler, having an adult temper tantrum. I'm embarrassed to see this ugliness surface, but it's true.

Please forgive me for being quick to blame or pick up the phone to complain to a friend. Please draw me to vent to You first, to bring my frustrations and safely process in Your presence. Thank You for accepting all of me—even the parts that need pruning and shaving of selfishness.

Where do I need to control my tongue? My emotions? My reactions? Speak to me about how I can practice self-control. Thank You for the grace You pour out as I yearn to be molded into Your likeness.

For the Spirit God gave us does not make us timid,
but gives us power, love and self-discipline.
2 TIMOTHY 1:7 NIV

The Healing Side of Silence

In my younger years, silence scared me. Words affirmed and told me I was on the right track. In maturity, God, please invite me to see silence as a chance to hear from You. I long to know what Your voice sounds like—and I can't if I'm constantly distracted with noise, media, or voices filling the room and my thoughts.

Your silence is where I can learn to discern my own thoughts and Yours. What do You wish to say today? Perhaps I need to carve out quiet to simply be with You. To sit in Your love and feel it down to my bones. To saturate myself in the Psalms and accept this space of silence as sacred ground. However You wish to meet me, I am here. Open and listening. God, forgive me for being afraid of what silence brings. Please show me the healing side of silence now.

It is good that one should wait quietly for the salvation of the Lord.
LAMENTATIONS 3:26 ESV

The Great Healer

God, there are pains that I thought had healed, and out of nowhere, *pop!* They surface! I'm left wondering what happened and what I could have done differently.

I recognize healing is a continual process. Would You search my heart and offer insight into where I need to accept and confess responsibility? Where do I need to forgive? How do I need to grow? And the ache of pain that still exists—Lord, would You please heal those tender places? Would You bring people to speak love and grace into the parts that are deeply wounded? Would You speak truth and help me lay down the lies I'm falsely believing or the extra weight I no longer need to carry?

You are the Great Healer, and my soul aches for Your restoration. I ask You to meet me in this continual healing journey. May I lean on You when the pain is too great and rest in Your unconditional arms of love.

The LORD appeared to us in the past, saying: "I have loved you with an everlasting love; I have drawn you with unfailing kindness."
JEREMIAH 31:3 NIV

A Spark of Fun and Laughter

God, I could use some fun in my life. Some laughter and joy and a spark of hope. What is clouding the joy and stealing the celebration of today? Help me stay here long enough to ponder the deeper places of my heart and pull out the melancholy parts.

You don't ask me to get rid of my authentic emotions or stitch on a fake smile. You desire true life to bubble out of me, and I desperately want that. Please nudge me toward what will bring a sense of fun today. A nature walk? Baking? Going out with a friend? Tackling a creative project?

You know me best. I bring my bad attitude to You now and thank You for welcoming all of me. Invite me to note the spark of fun You long to join me in, and give me tenacity to embrace it with passion and curiosity. For You are a Father who is fun and loves to delight in Your daughter.

So, whether you eat or drink, or whatever
you do, do all to the glory of God.
1 Corinthians 10:31 esv

Connecting Piece

God, I miss my brother. I hate that we live far away. I miss his funny voices and my sister-in-law and our niece and nephew. I miss spontaneous weekday dinners and playing in the front yard. I miss deep conversations on our couch and watching our kids play together.

Yet, in my missing him, God, help me not forget that we chose to move. That we felt stirred to step into a new state. Help me take advantage of the moments I miss him, to pray for him. To encourage him. To remind him of what a gift he is and how much he impacts my life, even from thousands of miles away.

God, please use this time we are apart to deepen my dependence on You. To transform my longings to be satisfied in Your intimate love and nearness. You are present whether I live there or here. Your boundaries surpass zip codes and time zones. Please bring my brother to mind often and offer discernment for how to pray and point him back to You as our connecting piece.

For he will not much remember the days of his life
because God keeps him occupied with joy in his heart.
ECCLESIASTES 5:20 ESV

A Tender Spirit

Lord, I'm used to how I do things. How I think. How I feel. So much *I, I, I*. I confess my comfortable ways and offer myself to You now. Please forgive me for being too rigid at times, too stubborn.

How can I tender my spirit? My will? My habits? My thoughts? What coping mechanisms need to be shaved off for surrender to be put in their place? Where are You inviting me to be malleable to Your will?

I offer my stubbornness and ask You to make me tender. Sensitive to Your Spirit. Willing to change my ways and listen more and speak less. Where do I need to soften? Let go? Shift directions? Please offer Your Spirit-breathed discernment and strength to soften the edges of my heart that have become hard. Mold me to be more like You, Jesus.

"Flesh gives birth to flesh, but the Spirit gives birth to spirit. You should not be surprised at my saying, 'You must be born again.' The wind blows wherever it pleases. You hear its sound, but you cannot tell where it comes from or where it is going. So it is with everyone born of the Spirit."
JOHN 3:6–8 NIV

Knowing Hope

I'm finding myself saying and thinking, *I know*. But here's my truth: there's much I don't know. God, please forgive me for my pride when I'm quick to judge what I do know and what others don't. My knowledge is a gift, and what comes easy to me may not come easy to others.

In the same way, please make me teachable to learn and ask questions and admit my lack of knowledge in the areas I want to grow. Help me lead with humility and an openness to learn. Protect my mind from shame, and cover me with the knowledge that to be human is to be dependent. How freeing this truth is. There's much beauty in admitting, *I don't know*. God, please turn my spirit to be taught by You, the One who knows all things and makes Yourself known.

May the God of hope fill you with all joy and peace in believing,
so that by the power of the Holy Spirit you may abound in hope.
ROMANS 15:13 ESV

Coffee Time

Today is a new day, and as I pour myself a cup of coffee, may I quiet myself before You, Lord. Help me offer You the first morning moments and find truth in Your Word.

What verses are You drawing me to? What are You saying today? What do I need to put aside so I can come, expectant and open, before You? What are the longings and desires of my heart? How are You inviting me to pray?

Please quiet my soul and use this coffee time to create a morning rhythm where I bring myself to You and allow You to fill me before I work, parent, create, and beyond.

As I pour my coffee, I imagine You pouring my being to the fullness of Your grace, Your love, Your power. As I drink my coffee, may I take quiet moments to prepare my heart to move about my day staying filled by You and refilling when I find my strength low and in need of Your renewed presence.

The steadfast love of the LORD never ceases; his mercies never come to an end; they are new every morning; great is your faithfulness.
LAMENTATIONS 3:22–23 ESV

Honest Breaths

Lord, please give me Your breath today. I'm exhaling heavy breaths of worry, anxiety, pride, and judgment. I'm breathing out jealousy, comparison, doubt, fear, and shame. I give all these honest breaths to You.

Help me, Lord, to breathe in Your truths: Your patience, love, peace, grace, beauty, and awareness. Help me breathe in forgiveness of self and others. Help me breathe in sensitivity to Your voice, Your movements, Your invitations. Help me breathe in purity of thoughts, words, and actions. Help me breathe in compassion, truth, mercy, and steadfastness.

I breathe out anything that's not of You and breathe in all that is of You—of light, of purity, of beauty. Forgive me for taking breaths for granted. Spirit of the living God, breathe afresh on me now.

"This is what the Sovereign LORD says to these bones:
I will make breath enter you, and you will come to life."
Ezekiel 37:5 NIV

....

....

....

....

....

....

....

....

....

A Stir to Experience

Lord, I'm becoming aware of how I enter conversations and circumstances for what I will take *from* them, instead of simply experiencing. Forgive me for my focus on self-benefit, instead of on the sheer joy of being and sitting in awe of a new friendship, a conversation, a beautiful moment.

I confess my rushed mind-set and ask You to transform my anxiousness to achieve. In its place, please stir me to experience. Experience You. Experience a new way I'm alive. Experience a new perspective. Experience the quiet. Experience fresh colors, smells, sounds, and textures.

What is life if not experienced? What is faith if not known? What is having access to a relationship with You if not noticed? Experience is my prayer. You are who I want to meet at every turn today.

*"And I will ask the Father, and he will give you another advocate to
help you and be with you forever—the Spirit of truth. The world
cannot accept him, because it neither sees him nor knows him.
But you know him, for he lives with you and will be in you."*
John 14:16–17 NIV

Confession of Apathy

God, my desire is diminishing. Desire for intimacy, desire for more, desire for anything. I'm tired and have nothing to give anyone. Would You show me how You are offering intimacy with me even if I have no energy to move toward You or anyone else? I feel like I'm letting down my husband, my kids, my friends—even myself. I feel untethered to all people.

I confess my apathy to You. God, will You please fan the flame of intimacy anew? Perhaps not how it was before, but in a restored, transformed way? What do I need to release? Surrender? Confess? Where am I critical when I need compassion? How can I look at others with grace instead of judgment? Where do I need to take ownership of my choices? Where do I need to be responsible for my voice and actions and step confidently into where You are stirring?

One thing I ask from the LORD, this only do I seek: that I may dwell in the house of the LORD all the days of my life, to gaze on the beauty of the LORD and to seek him in his temple.
PSALM 27:4 NIV

Craving Calm

God, I woke from a horrible dream that triggered a painful experience. What was that about? Where did that come from? I'm not sure, but what I do know is that my spirit feels unsettled.

Will You please meet me right now? As I note my heart pounding fast, where do I need to offer my painful memories? Where are You healing and offering love as I continually offer up my brokenness?

I confess my need for calm—a calm only You can offer. On my own, Lord, I'm anxious and full of worry.

Where in this dream were You? If I go back and imagine, where do I notice Your presence? Forgive me for neglecting to know You are near, even when painful moments spark. Please use this dream, God, to show me that You are with me in my pain—awake and asleep.

In peace I will both lie down and sleep; for you alone,
O Lord, make me dwell in safety.
Psalm 4:8 esv

Honest or Impressive?

God, I heard a friend ask, "Do you want to be honest or impressive?" My response? Both. I want to be honest *and* impressive. Even though I want to be honest, I still want the public validation of being impressive too.

I'm not proud of this, but I'm being honest with You. And You know my heart. So, God, please help me stand in my space and tell my truth and care more about being whole and true than impressive and adored.

At the same time, Lord, would You please remind me that because I am made in Your image, I am already impressive because *You* are impressive. I am impressive, not because of my accomplishments or boasting abilities, but because Your Spirit dwells in my being and I carry You wherever I go. Help me draw from Your truth and think, speak, and live honestly with a sincerity of spirit, caring more about Your thoughts than how others perceive me.

Righteous lips are the delight of a king,
and he loves him who speaks what is right.
PROVERBS 16:13 ESV

Avoidance of Sincerity

I find myself leading with sarcasm and wit in place of sincerity. I peer deeper and realize I'm avoiding sincerity because I'm more comfortable being funny than serious.

Why is this, Lord? What's in me that I feel like I need to be witty or funny when I truly want to connect? What's keeping me from taking off my humorous mask and letting myself be fully known and seen when there's no humor to cover myself with?

I repent of my lack of maturity and ask for bravery to be sincere. Would You tug my spirit when I fall back into well-worn paths of joking and needing a laugh? Help me discern when this is appropriate and when I'm avoiding an invitation for deep, real connection. Please give me courage to unmask and lead with sincerity.

Help me pay attention to my motives. What true parts emerge when I'm wholehearted? What does it mean to be heartfelt? What am I hiding? Help me start fresh today.

For we are not, like so many, peddlers of God's word, but as men of sincerity, as commissioned by God, in the sight of God we speak in Christ.
2 Corinthians 2:17 esv

Beauty All Around

Lord, I feel the need for beauty deep down in my bones. I need a hint of eternity, of rainbow sunsets, of butterflies and vibrant fields, of pure, raw beauty. How easy it is to go about my day and overlook Your beauty invitations: in the faces of my kids, the hug of my spouse, the playfulness of our puppy, the blooming flowers, the colorful skies, and even the designs on my shirt and the fun texture of my boots.

Forgive me, God, when I bypass beauty. Please invite me to pause and look up and around and down. Help me see beauty in Your people.

Where is beauty today? God, I'm on a mission to notice and reflect and to invite others to do the same.

The heavens declare the glory of God; the skies proclaim the work of his hands. . . . Their voice goes out into all the earth, their words to the ends of the world. In the heavens God has pitched a tent for the sun. . . . It rises at one end of the heavens and makes its circuit to the other; nothing is deprived of its warmth.
PSALM 19:1, 4, 6 NIV

Hunger for Truth

I'm becoming aware of my hunger for truth. For real, black-and-white, scriptural, I-feel-lighter-inside truth. Truth that comes only from You. Authentic. Pure.

I apologize, Lord, for my ease to accept as truth much of what I hear or read. I even make assumptions about my worth based on others' response to me instead of going to You first.

Turn my heart now and stir me toward truth. Where do I need to turn off untruthful voices and noise and turn on Your truth filter? Where in Your Word are You beckoning me to read and stay? What truth are You filling my mind, eyes, and heart with? What untruths have I been believing? Where are You longing to replace these lies with the reality of Your unconditional love? Lead me to Your truth, which is everlasting and freeing, indeed.

Do your best to present yourself to God as one approved,
a worker who does not need to be ashamed and
who correctly handles the word of truth.
2 TIMOTHY 2:15 NIV

All the Answers

God, I want control. I want to know how life will unfold. I want to have answers for all my questions. How long do I have to wait? What is Your plan? Why am I sitting in the quiet? Where is Your Spirit beckoning?

Do You hear all my questions and the anxiety underneath? Forgive me, God, for worrying—for clinging to answers more than Your presence. Draw me to curl up with You now. To simply be with You and enjoy Your presence, not for the answers I get, but for the intimacy that comes from sitting with You. Where I'm anxious for answers, please whisper that You are the answer—that You know my needs and will take care of me.

I surrender my control. I surrender my angst. I surrender my worry and frantic anxiety. I surrender my need to rush to the next answer before waiting for You to respond. I surrender my security in needing to have a plan. I surrender to You.

Humble yourselves before the Lord, and he will exalt you.
JAMES 4:10 ESV

A Nonjudgmental Heart

Ew. Just ew. God, I notice judgment surfacing in my thoughts, in my body language, in my tone of voice. I even see judgment restricting where love longs to live. Judgment is stifling any love that You want to shine from me. I notice this sin and confess my judgment to You now.

Why do I feel better than others in this way? What am I trying to prove? How can I learn and offer compassion, as opposed to lording my ways or pushing my opinion? Please remind me that You love every person the same. You love the way You created me and also love how You created the very person I am judging.

How can I make space for relationship with those who think, live, and love differently? How can I see You in this person I'm prone to judge? In place of judgment, I ask for compassion and unconditional love. Please burn Your love deep within me so that it will not go out.

You, therefore, have no excuse, you who pass judgment on someone else, for at whatever point you judge another, you are condemning yourself, because you who pass judgment do the same things.
ROMANS 2:1 NIV

Created to Create

God, I feel numb and void of creativity. Why am I stuck? What's blocking me from living out my truest self and pulling from You, my Creator? Help me be still and pay attention to what is keeping me from living alive. Stir me, please, toward what gives life.

Nature? Painting? People? Where am I most alive in Your presence? What is it You created me to create? Please invite me to notice Your movement and to praise You for the small ways You nudge me forward to make and play and do from a space of overflow.

May I notice You all around—in the sky, the voices, the work, the people, the challenges, the beauty. What colors awaken my soul? What textures? Sounds? Flavors?

Where are You repeating Yourself in conversations? In books? In scripture? May I be aware that this is You beckoning me toward living creative and free and full of Your work on display. For this I am thankful.

"He has filled them with skill to do all kinds of work as engravers, designers, embroiderers in blue, purple and scarlet yarn and fine linen, and weavers—all of them skilled workers and designers."
EXODUS 35:35 NIV

Sacred Communion

God, in the simplest of tasks, I give You praise! Even in the hustle-bustle of grocery shopping and checking pasta, tomato sauce, and basil off the list, I want to experience delight in You. Often You spoke in parables about the beauty of breaking bread and eating together. You manifest in bread, wine, fish, and miracles.

This meal I'm shopping for and will later prepare is a miracle. Forgive me for rushing past the sacredness of making dinner and feeding my people—their bellies and hearts. While we eat off chipped dishes and make messes, we know You are at the table with us. You are preparing the table even while the pasta is still simmering. You are preparing our hearts before we sit to share about our day. May we be mindful that dinner is not another time to eat, but a sacred invitation to pull up a chair and join You for communion. Thank You, Lord, for every bite.

Then Jesus declared, "I am the bread of life. Whoever comes to me will never go hungry, and whoever believes in me will never be thirsty."
JOHN 6:35 NIV

Collection of Tears

God, tears come quick and often today. I'm not sure what's at the root of them, but clearly they need to come out. Where are You turning the faucet on to bring deeper healing?

Help me allow my tears to flow; help me know You are holding me as I cry. You are not ashamed of my tears. You don't tell me to toughen up or wipe them away. You catch each one and store them up and know for every tear, a tender space is being brought to the surface that needs Your healing touch.

Please meet me here where my tears and heart overflow. Are tears a gateway to Your voice? Are they a connecting bridge to tenderness? Are tears a path toward trust? As each tear falls, I'm mindful that they carry a story, a wound, a need. I trust You know what my tears represent and will comfort me in a personal, tangible embrace. Hold me, Lord.

You've kept track of my every toss and turn through the sleepless nights, each tear entered in your ledger, each ache written in your book.
PSALM 56:8 MSG

Chosen

God, I ran into a former employer and felt a familiar thread course through me: I felt unpicked. Unchosen. Passed by. She saw my heart and talents and intentionally discarded me.

I'm hurt. Please tether me to Your truth. Forgive me for allowing this person to make me doubt, even for a second, that I'm chosen. You choose me. You pick me. You see me in a crowd and run to find me. You value me, for I am wonderfully and fearfully made. I am enough. My identity is steadfast in You.

Please whisper these truths over and over to my hurt heart today. Where I feel passed by, would You bring to mind moments when You chose me? When others chose me?

For every lie that is on a repeat reel, I ask You to replace it with a deep confidence, knowing that You choose me. Today. Tomorrow. Always. Despite how I act or when I mess up. Your love is void of my actions. My identity is safe and secure when I rest in You. Thank You, Jesus.

"And you will feel secure, because there is hope;
you will look around and take your rest in security."
Job 11:18 esv

73

Think On Your Thoughts

Lord, I'm sitting with Psalm 139 and the mind-blowing reality that You know my thoughts even before I do. This is cray-zee! Because, let's be honest, there are a lot of thoughts in this brain of mine. What's even more amazing is that You, the Maker of All, think about *me*.

So I'm curious, what *do* You think about me? What are Your thoughts toward me? How do You see me? What makes You laugh? What is entirely unique about how You formed my being? My soul? My passions? My story? I'm offering myself space to listen before I rush to think.

In place of my own thoughts, would You please allow me to peer into Your thoughts? To pay attention to where You are transforming and inviting me to deeper surrender? May my thoughts be more aligned to Yours. I offer this discipline to You today and ask, "What do You think about me, Lord?"

"For my thoughts are not your thoughts, neither are your ways my ways,"
declares the LORD. "As the heavens are higher than the earth, so are my
ways higher than your ways and my thoughts than your thoughts."
ISAIAH 55:8–9 NIV

A Teachable Spirit

There are projects I'm working on, and I confess, I feel dumb. I often find myself feeling confused and unsure of how to move forward. Lord, please use this project to mold a teachable spirit in me.

Where can I grow? How can I challenge myself to learn a complicated procedure, process, or project? How can I use this newly learned skill in the future? Where I'm quick to pile shame high on my shoulders for not understanding, will You please release this heavy load and whisper, *"I am proud of you, Daughter. You are stepping into a vulnerable space, and I see you. You are brave and imperfect and human."*

Please give me perseverance and tenacity to learn in confidence and humility. Fill my mind and heart with teachable questions and a spirit to learn. Make me a lifelong student. Of You. Of others. Of challenges. This is where You do beautiful work, Lord.

I have been crucified with Christ. It is no longer I who live, but Christ
who lives in me. And the life I now live in the flesh I live by faith
in the Son of God, who loved me and gave himself for me.
GALATIANS 2:20 ESV

Active Listening

Lord, I have a dear friend who is struggling with much. Her heart is overwhelmed and sad, and she is seeking guidance and help. I find myself wanting to rescue her, to ease her pain, to give her a verse and watch her move past this struggle.

Yet, I am not the Holy Spirit. You are. Forgive me for acting as You do—trying to problem-solve and fix her. She is not broken. She is beautifully in process. Please stir me to listen. And listen some more. Help me bite my lip when I'm tempted to advise, even with pure intentions. May deep, active listening pave my time with her.

May I ask questions that point back to seeking You. May I put myself aside. Please calm any anxious thoughts that surface in me, so that I may simply note them and then offer her my full attention. As I listen, may I visualize Your ear tuned wholly and completely to both of us.

If one gives an answer before he hears,
it is his folly and shame.
PROVERBS 18:13 ESV

Source of All Love

You are the source of all love. Anything that reflects love, is in love, or creates love is Yours, God. Love is fullness of light and wonder and beauty. In You there is no darkness or heaviness or shame.

Where do I see love in me? Where am I living through Your love and living loved as a result? Where am I carrying darkness that isn't mine to carry? Forgive me for paying more attention to the existence of darkness, rather than walking confidently in the light.

Lord, my heart cry is this: Where and how can I step fully into Your love today? Where do I resist Your love? Why? Where do I have a hard time allowing all of me to be loved? What's this about? Where do I readily receive Your love? May I bask in the light of Your love and not feel pressure to do anything with it other than humbly receive.

Whoever does not love does not know God, because God is love.
1 John 4:8 niv

Unfolding

Something within is unfolding. There's a deep interior work happening, and I feel compelled to share this with You, Lord. My honest response? I want to curl up and cave in—to fold up and in like a bed sheet.

Unfolding feels scary and vulnerable. Like the hidden parts of me are exposed and laid bare. Yet, I sense this is what trusting You looks like, journeying toward living unfolded and open. God, what is happening as I unfold? What are You asking me to unprotect from? What hidden parts of my heart are You healing? Where is Your light shining on dark places? How does unfolding open myself to Your Spirit? Your movement? Your voice?

God, I confess my fear and ask You for courage. Give me courage as I unfold one layer at a time.

We have spoken freely to you, Corinthians; our heart is wide open.
You are not restricted by us, but you are restricted in your own
affections. In return (I speak as to children) widen your hearts also.
2 Corinthians 6:11–13 esv

Be Still and Trust

Lord, I notice my constant need to defend and explain my opinion and decisions. "Do you see my perspective?" I grasp. And deeper, I notice how exhausted all the shielding makes me. I'm tired of defending how, when, and why I make the choices I do.

Why do I do this, God? What's underneath my hurried rush to justify? What if instead, I hand over my choices to You? How will this change me from within? Will this deep, still knowing root a quiet calm?

To live without defense, this is my heartbeat. God, forgive me for needing to be right. Awaken me to the truth that You are my Defender. You are fighting for me and with me. I need only be still. And trust. And know that You are God.

God shows his love for us in that while we were still sinners, Christ died for us. Since, therefore, we have now been justified by his blood, much more shall we be saved by him from the wrath of God. . . . More than that, we also rejoice in God through our Lord Jesus Christ, through whom we have now received reconciliation.
Romans 5:8–9, 11 esv

For Those in Need

God, at the stoplight, I saw a man asking for money. The poor. They are among us. Remind me, Lord, that I am no different. I am one natural disaster, financial upset, or tragedy away from being poor. Convict my heart to be tender toward the poor. Even more, please lead me to share my poorness of spirit with others. Encourage me to bravely share where I lack, where I'm without, where I'm in need, and how I desperately need You.

Whether poor financially, spiritually, or circumstantially, we are all poor. We just dress our poorness differently. Where is my poorness a gift? You long for us to be among the poor and the broken in spirit, for we know what it is to live in plenty or want and find our beings enough in You alone.

Please remind me of my poorness and others' poorness at every turn. Use these situations so I'll depend even more on You.

Do not withhold good from those to whom it
is due, when it is in your power to act.
PROVERBS 3:27 NIV

Spiritual Discernment

God, I feel full of anticipation. I sense You are moving me forward, but to what I'm not sure. When this happens, I feel doubt creep in. Do You really care? Do You see me? Do You really have big plans for me?

Much of my journey is one of slowing down and listening to Your voice, and I sense that tension of wanting to perform and simultaneously desiring to be still and small. How do I do both well? Please give me discernment and help me stay where Your peace is, where Your discerning presence is, where You are moving me toward a path everlasting.

Anything that distracts, threatens, or interrupts this space is not of You. Please give me awareness to turn and continue walking confidently toward Your grace. Forgive me, Lord, when I stay in my head and lose sight of Your work in me and through others. I ask for Spirit discernment today.

For the word of God is living and active, sharper than any two-edged sword, piercing to the division of soul and of spirit, of joints and of marrow, and discerning the thoughts and intentions of the heart.
HEBREWS 4:12 ESV

Under His Wings

God, in Psalm 91, You talk about covering me with Your wings. How can I slow down long enough to notice how You are over and around me? What does this feel like? Do I feel scared being hidden under the shadow of Your wings? Is it comforting? What are Your wings offering? Maybe protection? A safe shelter? What is it You are covering me from and for?

I confess I live from event to event and forget to pause and respond to how You are covering me. Please still me now to take notice. Help me to be mindful of what Your wings offer and to settle near You. God, would You please bring birds to my path today? Would You remind me of how present Your wings are and confetti them before and over and around me? Under Your span, I take refuge.

He will cover you with his feathers, and under his wings you will
find refuge; his faithfulness will be your shield and rampart.
Psalm 91:4 niv

Noticing the Gift of Quiet

Lord, when I pause and surrender to stillness and quiet, what are You saying? Do I make time to listen to Your voice? I admit, many times I take Your quietness for distance. I associate quietness with my own experience: people are quiet when they are mad, when they are acting passive-aggressively, when they are uncomfortable. I experience quietness from others, and their quietness feels heavy.

Your quietness though, Lord, is light. And safe. And flowing with peace. As You invite me to sit in Your quiet and familiarize myself with Your stillness, help me pay attention to the peace I experience. In Your quiet, there is no angry silence or passive-aggressive energy or intentional ignoring.

What are You offering in Your quiet? I will sit and listen and find comfort in being with You now.

"The LORD your God is in your midst, a mighty one who will save; he will rejoice over you with gladness; he will quiet you by his love; he will exult over you with loud singing."
ZEPHANIAH 3:17 ESV

Seeking Lovely

Lovely is what I'm seeking today. Lovely in spirit, in nature, in conversation, in You. Where are You drawing me to notice Your loveliness at home, in the sky, at work? A creative project? When working out? Is Your loveliness in gardening or reading or playing with my kids? Perhaps it's in designing a space or teaching or mowing the lawn.

Your loveliness, Lord, is it also in my broken places? In my pain and hurt and doubts and fears? Help me find Your loveliness in these places as well. Forgive me for closing the door on my ugly spaces and only looking for pretty. Pretty does not equal lovely. Lovely is what You are doing in all things—beautiful and messy. Lovely is the process of reflecting You. Please remind me of this when I'm quick to cover my ugly. Help me see all places objectively, as You see them—lovely to the core.

For by him all things were created, in heaven and on earth,
visible and invisible, whether thrones or dominions or rulers or
authorities—all things were created through him and for him.
And he is before all things, and in him all things hold together.
COLOSSIANS 1:16–17 ESV

Intentional Purpose

I'm a busy soul. I leave no margin for rest or breathing room on either side of my full calendar. Forgive me, God, for I feel in my body that this is not healthy. When I'm late I become crabby and resentful and angry. I am mad at. . . ? Who? Only I am in charge of my schedule! Here lies my challenge. I'm planning too much and frustrated when I'm exhausted come the end of the day.

Where are You inviting me to plan and live and create intentional space to breathe? Where am I scheduling time to be in Your presence? Am I blowing up the box I have You in and living open to how You breathe life into everyday, mundane tasks? In the cleaning and errands and driving, You are here.

Please help me not to waste another moment rushing frantic from one task to the next, but to live with intentional purpose and mindful awareness that You are with me. In all parts of my day.

The plans of the diligent lead surely to abundance,
but everyone who is hasty comes only to poverty.
PROVERBS 21:5 ESV

The Ultimate Answer

God, I don't get it. I don't understand what's happening in this season. Forgive me for feeling like I need to understand everything. I don't need to have all the answers, but to look to You as the ultimate Answer.

Why do I struggle with needing to understand and make sense and know? What's simmering beneath this? Forgive me, Lord, for making understanding an idol, one I worship more than the messy process of trusting You one moment at a time. Your ways are perfect. Help me trust this truth. Help me settle into knowing that You know all things. You understand everything. You have the full picture. You get it. Through and through. When I panic at my lack of understanding, would You please pull my face to Yours and whisper, *"I have you. And My understanding is enough and perfect and good. I've got you."*

Thank You, Jesus.

From heaven the LORD looks down and sees all mankind;
from his dwelling place he watches all who live on earth—
he who forms the hearts of all, who considers everything they do.
PSALM 33:13–15 NIV

Surrendering "Should"

There's a funny phrase, "Stop shoulding all over yourself." And I'm finding this to be true. When I catch myself saying I *should* do this, or I *should've* done that, I'm placing unspoken expectations on myself. *Should* is obligatory and heavy. *Should* covers shame. *Should* channels pressure. I confess this awareness to You, God, and ask for You to remove the word *should* from my everyday life. Please replace it with *I get to*.

I get to serve. I get to work. I get to love people. I get to say no. I get to say yes. I get to listen to You before anyone else and decide accordingly. I get to breathe life and hope where *should* chokes and suffocates. I get to live confidently instead of feeling like a victim of my life. Goodbye, *should*. Hello, *I get to*. Thank You for this heartfelt shift in how I speak, Lord.

"Give, and it will be given to you. Good measure, pressed down, shaken together, running over, will be put into your lap. For with the measure you use it will be measured back to you."
Luke 6:38 esv

87

Quiet Contemplation

God, I'm aware of how often I believe the lie that I need to be fun. What is this about? What would it look like for me to have fun without feeling like I need to embody fun all the time?

You, Lord, created my mind and brain to ponder and learn. You made me smart and with a purpose. I confess I focus on being fun instead of celebrating the deep, contemplative parts of me. What would it look like to allow myself to settle into a comfortable rhythm of being and thinking when I'm tempted to perform and embody fun?

I'm sorry for dismissing this way You made me. Help me draw my attention to how You meet me in the deeper contemplative spaces; help me find myself at rest. Thank You, Jesus, for loving the fun parts of me as well as the deep, emotional, and intellectual parts equally.

Praise awaits you, our God, in Zion; to you our vows will be fulfilled.
PSALM 65:1 NIV

Ever-Present Spirit

God, sometimes I forget to notice that You are always with me. When I am sad, You are with me. Joyful? You are with me. You tell me that if I go to the heavens, You are there. And to the depths of the earth, You are still with me. I love that You are a constant companion, a friend as well as my Savior.

God, please forgive me for neglecting this truth. For mistaking Your intimacy for a feeling. You are with me even when I can't feel You. Even when I'm walking through the valley, Your Spirit is ever present. I'm quieting myself now to listen. Help me notice the movement of Your Spirit in this moment. In this day. In my comings and goings and thoughts and questions. Awaken me to how personal and near and constant Your Spirit is in and through me.

I'm so grateful that You are a God I don't have to go to. You draw near and stay with me. Through every moment.

And he said to them, "Pay attention to what you hear:
with the measure you use, it will be measured to you,
and still more will be added to you."
MARK 4:24 ESV

Source of Truth

I did it again. I argued because I have this horrible habit of needing to be right, and then making everyone around me aware of just how right I am. I defend and argue and make my opinion known. Why? Why do I have to be right? What about simply living true?

Please forgive me, God, for the anxiousness of having to defend my decisions. I heard a wise man once say that to live a life of defenselessness is where peace abounds. How true this is. You are my Defender. You are the source of truth. May I settle into this and know I don't need to justify, but simply live from a place of trueness.

Where I'm quick to defend and argue, forgive me. Where I'm anxious to add an extra comment or thought, quiet my voice. Turn me instead to You. Please secure in me a deep awareness that I may possess knowledge without having to proclaim it for all to hear.

"You will know the truth, and the truth will set you free."
JOHN 8:32 ESV

This Pause

God, I feel like life is on pause. There's little movement or direction. I'm listening but unsure of how to move forward, or what to lean into. What happens in this pause? Fear. Anxiety. I can feel my blood pressure skyrocket and am tempted to kick into "go mode" simply to make any type of action occur.

Why do I do this? What scares me about being on pause? Please forgive me, Lord, for my impatience. What are You inviting me to notice, learn, or surrender in this in-between place? Where are You asking me to stay when I really just want to crawl out of my skin and make something happen?

Perhaps, Lord, the purpose of this pause isn't the next step but a greater intimacy with knowing You are here. You are in the middle of the "not-yet." You are in control of this pause, and for this reason alone I trust You.

I believe that I shall look upon the goodness of the Lord in the land of the living! Wait for the Lord; be strong, and let your heart take courage; wait for the Lord!
Psalm 27:13–14 esv

Chosen Today and Every Day

God, I feel rejected. Unchosen. Invisible. Like the kid who didn't get picked on the playground. Did You ever feel this way? You were rejected by Your hometown. The very people You grew up with tried to run You out. And my heart simultaneously breaks and finds comfort in knowing You understand.

Rejection is painful. But please help me not lose myself to shame. Forgive me for even entertaining the thought that because I've been rejected, I'm rejectable. This is not truth. This is not who I am or how You see me. I am chosen by You.

Please forgive me for assuming there's a flaw in me, a reason for this rejection. Turn my heart to the truth that perhaps You are protecting me in this circumstance. You are teaching me compassion. You are reminding me that regardless of being chosen or unchosen, I am fearfully and wonderfully made.

As you come to him, a living stone rejected by men but in the sight of God chosen and precious, you yourselves like living stones are being built up as a spiritual house, to be a holy priesthood, to offer spiritual sacrifices acceptable to God through Jesus Christ.
1 Peter 2:4–5 esv

Focused Mind, Body, Spirit

Man, oh man, I feel all over the place. My mind is racing, and I can't finish one thought before another tumbles and crashes on top. My body feels on edge, and I can't focus.

Thank You for making me aware of my hamster-wheel mind-set. Lord, I ask You to help me focus now. What is it You are saying? Where can I devote my attention and time? Please clear away all extra thoughts and speak directly and clearly and in a way that I can part the cloud of confusion and come face-to-face with my Creator. Calm my whirlwind thoughts, and like You did to Job, speak from Your whirlwind to my anticipating soul.

Please focus my mind, spirit, and body to Your Spirit now.

Blessed is the one who does not walk in step with the wicked or stand in the way that sinners take or sit in the company of mockers, but whose delight is in the law of the LORD, and who meditates on his law day and night. That person is like a tree planted by streams of water, which yields its fruit in season and whose leaf does not wither—whatever they do prospers.
PSALM 1:1–3 NIV

His Capable, Loving Arms

God, my children are struggling. I confess I want to run and scoop them up and rescue them from any and all pain. I want to wrap a heart Band-Aid around their soul and assure them that everything will be fine. But I don't know the future. Only You know all and see all. And to know that You see my children and know their thoughts before they even fully form them brings this mama comfort.

I surrender my children to You. I surrender my longing to protect and assure and shield them, and I rest them in Your capable, loving arms.

God, I ask for mama discernment. Please tender me to their needs so that I can be a physical reminder of Your unconditional love and reflect You to them while they are in my care.

"All your children will be taught by the Lord,
and great will be their peace."
Isaiah 54:13 niv

A Driving Conversation

Lord, I hopped in the car, just as I do every day, and realized, *I take this thing for granted.* I take for granted that I can shimmy over to the grocery store or to the drive-through for coffee. I take for granted that I can get where I need to be in a safe vehicle.

What if a tire suddenly blows or the brakes go out? Will I be frustrated at this inconvenience? Absolutely! And for this I apologize and ask forgiveness. For You are the Giver of good gifts. This car. This gas. These people I carry to sports practices. A trunk that holds groceries and goodies.

As I drive, God, I ask You to transform this time into worship. Help me turn off all noise and distractions and listen to You. Stir me to pray and ponder and pay attention to what's happening inside. Transform my driving time into a beautiful prayerful conversation with You.

Be not quick in your spirit to become angry,
for anger lodges in the heart of fools.
Ecclesiastes 7:9 esv

Celebrating Christ's Birth

Christmas is a celebration. A celebration of life and all the tiny details making up the story of Your birth. Yet, I'm struck by the irony, as I'm surrounded by gifts and wrapping paper, that much of this season becomes about the gifts, instead of seeing You as the ultimate gift.

I'm sorry for getting caught up in the buying and wrapping and stress of holidays and neglecting to savor the lead-up to what Christmas celebrates. I am so thankful, Father, that You had the divine idea to bring Jesus to earth as a baby, a pure, innocent baby, born in a lowly barn. You turned the idea of a king upside down then and have ever since.

Forgive me for idolizing the wrapping, and bring me to the awareness of Your incarnate being this season.

So they hurried off and found Mary and Joseph, and the baby, who was lying in the manger. When they had seen him, they spread the word concerning what had been told them about this child, and all who heard it were amazed at what the shepherds said to them. But Mary treasured up all these things and pondered them in her heart.
Luke 2:16–19 niv

My Honest, Present Self

All right, Lord. I'm downright irritable and crampy and cranky. I want to lie in bed all day and watch the Hallmark channel and eat *all* the chocolate. And instead of beating myself up for this, help me turn my PMS-y attitude into a celebration of being a woman. You love women, and You love this woman. You respect and see our strength. I love how it was Mary who first saw You after You rose from the dead. It was women You showed Yourself to; You broke all cultural boundaries and loved them dearly.

And You love me right now—just as I am. Forgive me for feeling like I need to bring You my best, my shiny, my everything-is-great attitude. You don't want fake. You want my honest, present self. So, I'm bringing my real self to You now and trusting that Your unconditional love longs to be near me, even when I'm PMS-y.

She dresses herself with strength and makes her arms strong. She perceives that her merchandise is profitable. Her lamp does not go out at night.
PROVERBS 31:17–18 ESV

Slow to Speak

Forgive me, God, for I am having trouble staying silent. I interrupt and share unsolicited advice. I try to steer and manipulate people to what I think is best for them instead of encouraging them to listen to Your voice. What affirmation am I looking for in this? Deeper still, what discomfort is bubbling up so that I'm struggling to allow others to be on their individual journeys?

Silence is my prayer. Please forgive me when I am slow to speak. I long to listen deeply and well without forming thoughts while another speaks. Silence—to listen to You, to listen to myself, and to listen to others. Silence is a healing gift when people need to be heard. Would You gently invite me to practice silence when I'm tempted to speak? Will You please remind me of times You are silent and the gift You offer in that space? Please give me self-control to follow Your lead as I tuck words close and listen closer.

Know this, my beloved brothers: let every person
be quick to hear, slow to speak, slow to anger.
JAMES 1:19 ESV

Still Good

I've been thinking lately about healing. About how we, as believers, pray for healing. What about the times when healing isn't on this side of heaven? Is that still *healing*? What is *true* healing? God, I confess I selfishly pray for people to be healed. For suffering to end. For illnesses to disappear. For cancer to be erased. Why do horrible diseases and tragedies happen? Where are You in these circumstances?

I bring these honest questions to You and trust You can handle them. Know my heart, Lord, and please draw me to find security in You alone. God, perhaps my prayer for healing is an invitation to find my longings fulfilled in eternity with You. Where there is no sickness. Until then, please give me boldness to pray and trust that You heal in out-of-the-box ways. I don't always have to understand to know that You are still good.

Lord, by such things people live; and my spirit finds life in them too.
You restored me to health and let me live. Surely it was for my benefit
that I suffered such anguish. In your love you kept me from the pit
of destruction; you have put all my sins behind your back.
ISAIAH 38:16–17 NIV

True Transformation

God, I realize I hide behind blaming. Blaming the people around me. Blaming everyone else for my choices. Yet, I am the only one responsible for my choices—regardless of what anyone has done to me. I see my natural bent is to hide behind my pain instead of coming out from behind this false protection, willing to be vulnerable and seen. Will You forgive me, Lord, for using other people to keep me from freedom and healing? Will You give me courage to put down this self-protection mechanism so I can stand exposed and ready to receive?

Will You please impart wisdom in how to move forward, when for so long I've grown accustomed to taking the posture of sitting and blaming? Help me trust You for healing as I slowly lower my shield and take up Your promise of protection. I'm scared, but I know I must take this brave step in order to find true transformation.

The LORD is my strength and my shield; in him my heart trusts, and I am helped; my heart exults, and with my song I give thanks to him.
PSALM 28:7 ESV

"Right" vs. "Real"

God, the towel was on the floor, and my husband was trying to talk to me. But all I could focus on was the towel. Why is it that I see the imperfections instead of the people?

Lord, I'm sorry. I know at the root of this reaction is my need to be right. I want everyone else to see what I see and pick up the towels that are lying on the floor. I admit, I have little patience for those who are free-spirited and without a schedule. I become anxious and frustrated and don't understand how they don't follow a plan. Yet, maybe I can learn from their trusting, openhanded ways. Is there a lesson to learn in not needing to be right?

Help me stay honest to the ways You created me, while softening the hard edges that focus on being right where I really ought to be real.

Whoever walks in integrity walks securely,
but whoever takes crooked paths will be found out.
PROVERBS 10:9 NIV

Homesickness

God, I feel the ache of missing my old home and still not feeling 100 percent at home here. This middle ground is weird, and I admit, I'm unsure where "home" truly is. Would You please tether me to the truth that no matter what my zip code is, You are with me?

I can make myself at home with You, for You dwell in me. What are the aspects of my former home that I miss? Would You meet me in these spaces today?

What is it You are stirring in me as I hope for home? Guide me to a new perspective of what home is. Is it people? An area? Feeling known? May I look further to find respite in You, even as I miss what's behind and hold fast to the hope of what is ahead.

Jesus said, "Truly, I say to you, there is no one who has left house or brothers or sisters or mother or father or children or lands, for my sake and for the gospel, who will not receive a hundredfold now in this time, houses and brothers and sisters and mothers and children and lands, with persecutions, and in the age to come eternal life."
MARK 10:29–30 ESV

Flexible and Teachable

God, nothing is going as planned. Health. House emergencies. A change in work plans. When I find myself clinging to control and order, would You redirect me to notice how I can be flexible and teachable instead? Where do I need to surrender my plan for Yours?

Please forgive me for focusing on getting things done and neglecting to sit with You first. None of this comes as a surprise. I confess I don't need You until I do. And I need You now.

May my daily prayer be *God, I begin this day with intent. I trust that as I work and listen and hold my hands open in expectancy, You will not let me miss anything. May my focus be You and You alone.* Help me laugh when disruptions come and lean deeper into allowing small details to be just that: small.

I know how to be brought low, and I know how to abound. In any and every circumstance, I have learned the secret of facing plenty and hunger, abundance and need. I can do all things through him who strengthens me. Yet it was kind of you to share my trouble.
PHILIPPIANS 4:12–14 ESV

Time Investment

Much of my day seems governed by time. I watch the clock hands and feel a familiar twinge of rush. There seems to be an inner alarm clock threatening to go off when I entertain the idea of pausing. Forgive me for living on the edge of exhaustion.

God, I admit, the clock is my idol. I allow it to boss me around and steal my joy. Could it be, when I offer You my firsts, that You will maximize my hours? How will You set the time and give me what I need for today?

Please speak to me about where to invest my minutes and hours. I want to be in constant communication with You. Should I say yes to this? What about this? What will bring You the most glory? What can wait? . . .

I offer my time to You. Please help me steward the minutes and hours wisely.

Look carefully then how you walk, not as unwise but as wise, making the best use of the time, because the days are evil. Therefore do not be foolish, but understand what the will of the Lord is.
EPHESIANS 5:15–17 ESV

Help for Hurts

I confess I feel shame in admitting that my feelings are hurt. A mocking voice says, "Get tough skin; stop being so sensitive." Yet, I would be lying to say I'm not hurt. And I need You to help me heal from this hurt before I can move on. To shove it deeper or ignore it would be to keep myself from feeling and healing. God, what is at the root of this hurt? What about this pain is my part to learn from? What part is not mine to carry and therefore necessary to grieve?

I'm handing You my hurt. Would You turn it over and reveal to me what to grow from and what to leave behind? Even as my heart is sad, please be my comfort. Thank You for listening and holding me and accepting all my big emotions and honest feelings. Thank You for loving me in this fragile space. Please cover me, Lord. I need Your safe arms right now.

"The Lord will fight for you, and you have only to be silent."
Exodus 14:14 esv

Light in the Darkness

Anything that shimmers or hints of light is from You, Lord. Help me pay attention to this in my innermost being. Where is there peace? That's of You. Where is there joy? That's of You. Where is there a sense of feeling alive and whole? All of this beauty is from You.

I confess that I struggle to celebrate the light until it's dark. So I'm calling out my gratitude in the light and in the dark, for You are in all of it.

Where there is anxiety or lack of peace, help me turn toward Your light. Where there is shame or self-loathing, help me leave this behind. Where there is doubt and worry, let me lay this at Your feet. I only want to follow where You call my name and to believe this path is drenched in star-laden light.

*Again Jesus spoke to them, saying, "I am the light
of the world. Whoever follows me will not walk
in darkness, but will have the light of life."*
JOHN 8:12 ESV

Purity of Thought

God, I used to believe that pure thoughts were only those free of lust or sexual fantasies, but I'm discovering that purity of thought is also believing the best of myself, You, and others. Are my thoughts pure? Am I contemplating thoughts that are honest, authentic, and true?

Please forgive me when my thoughts are not pure. When they are tinged with doubt and a negative view. When I look for where someone (or myself) lacks and focus only on these shortcomings.

Turn my mind and heart toward pure thoughts; set my mind apart to trust, believe, and cling to what is beautiful and honest and sincere. Forgive my impure thoughts. And help me be gentle with myself when impure thoughts creep back in; gently remove them and keep them from becoming an inner narrative.

Finally, brothers and sisters, whatever is true, whatever is noble, whatever
is right, whatever is pure, whatever is lovely, whatever is admirable—
if anything is excellent or praiseworthy—think about such things.
Philippians 4:8 niv

Even as I Walk

God, as I walk up and down our street and notice the clouds and the birds and the flowers that are blooming and grass that is growing, may all of this be a whisper of Your creation. May I not pass by without noticing where You are seeding, uprooting, and showing Yourself in nature. God, thank You for the very legs that I walk on and my health. Forgive me for how easily I take this for granted. Even as I walk, would You strengthen my steps?

Continue to invite me forward to where You are growing me and tethering me deeper to Your Spirit and making me more discerning of Your voice. Thank You that You are a God who walks with, beside, behind, and in front of me. Thank You for hemming me in and companioning me right now, even as I walk.

Dear friend, I pray that you may enjoy good health and that all may go well with you, even as your soul is getting along well.
3 John 1:2 NIV

Advocacy

God, I feel like I need to be my own advocate, as well as my family's. I need to speak up so that I feel heard. I doubt and wonder, *Are You my Advocate?*

Where are You advocating for me? Where are You speaking on my behalf? How are You moving if I don't speak up? These are the questions I have, and these are the honest confessions I bring to You now.

I admit that I'm afraid that if I don't practice using my voice, I will become silent. And yet, You say that You fight for me, and so I'm asking, God, would You please be my Advocate? Would You please speak for and fight for and celebrate me when I so badly just want to be noticed and understood by others? Would You meet that need in a way only You can?

My little children, I am writing these things to you so that you may not sin. But if anyone does sin, we have an advocate with the Father, Jesus Christ the righteous.
1 John 2:1 esv

Responding with a Yes or No

God, I notice my tendency to react instead of to respond. To jump at the biggest need, the largest fire, and whoever is shouting the loudest. These needs are valid and important, yet it is not my job to be the rescuer or fix problems or provide for everyone's needs. Only You can do that.

I confess that often my identity comes from being the one who shows up, being the helper, having the right answer and the wise advice—and for this, I'm sorry. I'm sorry that my pride gets in the way.

Please be at the root of my responses. Stir me toward where You want me to say yes and where You want me to say no. May I stand courageously where You have me, where You want me to respond.

May I hold every need before You and think and pray and listen before I give an answer. I am thankful that You see all these needs. You know all these concerns. You hear every cry, and You are in all of this.

"Let what you say be simply 'Yes' or 'No';
anything more than this comes from evil."
MATTHEW 5:37 ESV

Cloud-Watching

God, I'm sitting on the porch, staring out at the horizon, mesmerized by the deep blue sky—like a canvas You're eagerly painting. I imagine You sit back, then dab to create a cloud wisp; with Your brush, a rainbow appears.

You offer up sunrises and sunsets and rainbows and rain, and all of this pleases You. God, I love Your creativity. How can I echo this in my day? How can I bring beauty to conversations and work spaces and even my wardrobe? How can I add color and brush moments with kindness? How can I take the peace of cloud-watching into my whole day?

God, even in my desire to embrace the beauty You make, please help me so that I don't feel like I have to mimic, but simply appreciate, Your works. Let me sit in awe of how You design; let me turn my face upward toward the clouds and smile.

"Do you know how God controls the clouds and makes his lightning flash? Do you know how the clouds hang poised, those wonders of him who has perfect knowledge?"
Job 37:15–16 NIV

111

Love Reminders

Love is such an ambiguous, big, simple word. Yet, what it contains is the undercurrent of unconditionality. You love unconditionally. You love me when I mess up. You love me when I try and fail. I know this well. I see Your personal reminders in heart shapes in the cream of my coffee. I see leaves scattered underfoot in the shape of hearts. God, I see hearts in makeup splatters, cement designs, and spills.

All of these reminders draw me back to love. You are love. You love me. I am loved unconditionally. And even when my soul struggles to understand this, would You please echo this in front of my eyes and bring my heart to scripture and truth so that the constant messaging that I'm saturated with is love? Deep, simple, unconditional love.

But you, Lord, are a compassionate and gracious God,
slow to anger, abounding in love and faithfulness.
Psalm 86:15 niv

Becoming

Sweet li'l caterpillar. I'm glad I was paying attention and saw it before I stepped on its cute furry body. You know what it reminded me of, God? *Becoming.* A caterpillar is in the process of becoming what it's supposed to be—it's a butterfly-in-waiting. And I am too. But so often all I see is the spiky, furry, climbing-on-the-ground, humble, mundane, invisible steps taken day after day.

God, may I be this caterpillar? May I delight in what I'm learning by being so near to the ground? So dependent on the vastness of what's above me? Because, God, when You do Your work in me and I become who You are making me to be, I will one day soar. Like a butterfly.

Give me patience, Jesus. Whether I'm crawling or soaring, thank You for who I am becoming and need to be.

And we all, with unveiled face, beholding the glory of the Lord, are being transformed into the same image from one degree of glory to another. For this comes from the Lord who is the Spirit.
2 Corinthians 3:18 esv

Staying in Peace

Lord, I find myself wanting to stay in this sanctuary space of peace where You dwell, and simultaneously wanting to burst through and take action. I want to make things happen and revert to old habits and say, "Look at me. Look at what I'm doing. Aren't I amazing and talented?" I'm sorry. I'm sorry I want to be seen by the world. And yet I know that leaving this space of peace isn't worth it because it forces me to do life on my own, instead of accepting the fact that Your peace is a gift that I can settle into.

God, I ask for Your strength when I'm tempted to leave this space of peace because of discomfort. May this discomfort be a bed of comfort. May I know You are near even as I hold the tension of wanting to leave this space and wanting to stay here forever. Help me find the balance, please.

Let the peace of Christ rule in your hearts, since as members
of one body you were called to peace. And be thankful.
Colossians 3:15 niv

Discerning the Gifts I've Asked For

God, I recently read a beautiful prayer about how when I ask for a gift, I also have to take responsibility for the gift You've given. So, I'm wondering, what is the gift that You've given me? How are You asking me to be responsible for it?

If I'm honest, God, I know this gift is one of quiet work and not of exterior show. Even in this, God, would You please talk to me like You did to Abraham? Would you echo Your words so that I can say, "I'm listening obediently to Your voice"? I'm trusting this gift is one I've asked for, and even though I don't understand how it's supposed to unfold, I'll continually walk obediently and willingly to where You call me.

Each of you should use whatever gift you have received to serve others, as faithful stewards of God's grace in its various forms. If anyone speaks, they should do so as one who speaks the very words of God. If anyone serves, they should do so with the strength God provides, so that in all things God may be praised through Jesus Christ. To him be the glory and the power for ever and ever. Amen.
1 Peter 4:10–11 niv

Lovely Autumn

The weather is changing. Summer is melting into crisp mornings and cool evenings, and the trees are putting on their orange coats. It's beautiful outside. God, please use this autumn season to help me make a new rhythm of stilling myself with You.

May the coldness help me curl up in the warmth of You first. May the chilly air beckon me to shorter days and more time inside, laughing, cozying up, and worshipping You as I make soup, snuggle with my family, and read books. All of fall is an autumn offering. A shift in weather invites a heart shift. Please draw me closer to You. With every fall tradition, will You please help me pay attention to what You are turning over in me?

You crown the year with your bounty;
your wagon tracks overflow with abundance.
Psalm 65:11 esv

A Prayer for Communication

God, I admit that as much as I'm trying to communicate clearly and listen actively, I'm missing the mark with some people. I'm sharing my honest feelings, even though I sense that my honesty will put them on the defense. Nevertheless, God, I ask for courage to share and stay tethered to Your Spirit, even when conflict occurs.

Please help me not shy away from hard conversations, but instead learn from them. Where do I get triggered? Why am I anxious? What am I afraid of? Where are You in this dialogue? Lord, I confess I'm not an expert at communication, but I am a follower of You. You are familiar with conflict and tension and didn't shy away from hard situations but spoke with love and listened.

Help me as I listen and share. Help me stay myself and be open to constructive feedback. Through our words, may You be glorified.

The words of the reckless pierce like swords, but the tongue of the wise brings healing. Truthful lips endure forever, but a lying tongue lasts only a moment. Deceit is in the hearts of those who plot evil, but those who promote peace have joy.
PROVERBS 12:18–20 NIV

When Others Expect Me to Carry Them

I had an awkward conversation with someone who figuratively threw all her stuff on my lap and then walked away. And when I kindly handed it back to her, she was angry and defensive.

God, I'm shocked at her expectations to be carried, and at the same time I understand. For so long, I used to carry her—emotionally, spiritually. I swooped in whenever she was in crisis to encourage, pray, and be present. But I realized this was not healthy for me. And so I had to instill boundaries—boundaries that You and I decided on.

Jesus, I need Your help forgiving her for pushing me to break my boundaries. I need compassion to care about her without having to carry her. I need confidence to be a friend but not her everything.

While he was still speaking to the people, behold, his mother and his brothers stood outside, asking to speak to him. But he replied to the man who told him, "Who is my mother, and who are my brothers?" And stretching out his hand toward his disciples, he said, "Here are my mother and my brothers! For whoever does the will of my Father in heaven is my brother and sister and mother."
MATTHEW 12:46–50 ESV

Uncomfortable People

God, I'm thankful that although I'm uncomfortable, You put people in my path who are different than I am so I can learn a different facet of who You are. If the image of You is in everybody (and it is), then I get to meet different facets of Your essence and Your perspective through others.

Forgive me for being quick to categorize or to assume I won't be friends with someone if there isn't an instant connection. Is there a part of my personality that needs to be softened by being around this person? Am I willing to do life and journey with those who are uncomfortable for me? In this discomfort, please help me find that the connection piece is You. You love all Your people the same, and there is beauty in learning from those that, with only one look, I may miss out on knowing.

"Why do you see the speck that is in your brother's eye, but do not notice the log that is in your own eye? Or how can you say to your brother, 'Let me take the speck out of your eye,' when there is the log in your own eye?"
MATTHEW 7:3–4 ESV

Forgiving a Family Member

Lord, I was honest when I shared with a family member that my feelings were hurt. This is growth for me. But when I shared, I was met with a defensive spirit, and I admit, God, it hurts. Even in my hurt, will You please help me be confident that my speaking up was indeed a step in being healthy and using the voice You've given me?

Will You please help me forgive? I realize that so often the way people respond isn't about me. Help me see through the defensive response and notice the hurt they are experiencing, how my words hit a personal area for them. Help me notice that it isn't my responsibility to bear the burden of their response emotionally, but to simply pray for them.

God, thank You for encouraging me to use my voice and be confident as I share my honest feelings.

Then Peter came up and said to him, "Lord, how often will my brother sin against me, and I forgive him? As many as seven times?" Jesus said to him, "I do not say to you seven times, but seventy-seven times."
MATTHEW 18:21–22 ESV

Tunnel Vision

Lord, I'm struck by how much of my community is married and have kids. Recently, a single friend said she has a hard time connecting with her married friends because much of their conversation centers around marriage and kids.

This gave me a fresh perspective to see those who are in a different life stage. God, forgive me for having tunnel vision. Help me focus on single souls who are longing to be married and have kids, or to be remarried. Forgive me for my selfishness in only seeing those who are in similar seasons.

Lord, would You please bring single friends to mind? Who is single and needs encouragement and comfort? How can I build a community that is young and old, single and married, childless and with children? May I create a community that echoes who You hold in heaven—one of every age and stage.

What, then, shall we say in response to these things? If God is for us, who can be against us? He who did not spare his own Son, but gave him up for us all—how will he not also, along with him, graciously give us all things?
Romans 8:31–32 niv

121

New Life

On a walk, I passed a sweet expectant mom-to-be. She's ripe with pregnancy. Oh, pregnancy. It's such a sweet season of anticipation and longing and eagerness to birth a babe. You know what, God? I didn't like being pregnant. I didn't like being uncomfortable and not being able to move or be as active. I'm sorry that sometimes I neglected to delight in this season. Yet, You are birthing something in me now. Even if it's not a baby, it may be a stirring or a dream or a longing. God, help me stay the course. Please give me patient endurance.

Even as I notice this expectant mom, may I delight in every stage of carrying, birthing, and knowing that new life comes every day.

"Before I formed you in the womb I knew you, before you were born
I set you apart; I appointed you as a prophet to the nations."
JEREMIAH 1:5 NIV

Living Awake

At church we read a prayer, and a few words connected to my soul: *open*, *empty*, *awake*. God, please help me live awake every day. Help me look for You in the details and people.

Where do You want me to live fully, with eyes open, palms out, and a heart surrendered to where Your Spirit is guiding and moving? God, where are You inviting me to live awake? Where am I sleepy or shut down?

God, I'm asking Your Spirit to gently pull back the covers and help me to my feet so that I may live awake. For when I live awake in Your Spirit, I live alive. And this is where You are glorified. So I ask: Where is Your attentive gaze drawing me to live awake? What does this look like today?

For anything that becomes visible is light. Therefore it says, "Awake,
O sleeper, and arise from the dead, and Christ will shine on you."
EPHESIANS 5:14 ESV

A Resistant Heart

Lord, I'm noticing where faith is beckoning me forward and where I'm resistant. Resistance comes in feeling tired or lethargic, or something in my spirit pushes back. I'm curious. What are You doing in these spaces of resistance, God? Is this protection? Is this confirmation? Are You helping me avoid something I shouldn't put mind and heart energy toward? Is this spiritual?

I know resistance isn't bad, but a choice to push through or resign. Would You give me discernment about if this resistance is from You? Or is this my ego avoiding? I ask for Your grace when I notice resistance. I confess that I'm human and don't see what You do. I trust You are lovingly journeying with me as I press onward toward a life lived in faith.

I delight in the law of God, in my inner being, but I see in my members another law waging war against the law of my mind and making me captive to the law of sin that dwells in my members. Wretched man that I am! Who will deliver me from this body of death? Thanks be to God through Jesus Christ our Lord!
Romans 7:22–25 esv

A Humble Spirit

God, it wasn't long ago that our family was almost homeless. Money was tight, and I scrounged for quarters in the car. Now that we're in a season of respite and breathing room, God, please help the poor be ever near my heart. I apologize for almost having a pity posture when I see the poor. Yet, I know how quickly a job loss or a tragedy or a natural disaster can bring us back to that poor space. More than anything, today I'm grateful that our season of being poor is at bay. I'm celebrating this season of breathing and grace.

I know that having once been poor attunes me to be mindful that the poor are always near and that is where You are. Help me carry the cadence of a poor, humble spirit into every situation today. Thank You, Jesus.

A righteous man knows the rights of the poor;
a wicked man does not understand such knowledge.
PROVERBS 29:7 ESV

Growth

God, I notice that in order to grow, I have to put down something to pick up something new. With this comes grief. I grieve what no longer fits, what I'm outgrowing. Lord, would You please continue speaking to me about what needs to die so that my spirit can hold the new work You are doing?

What coping mechanisms, habits, or comforts are You inviting me to put down? Where are You inviting me into a new way of living? I apologize for beating myself up for feeling embarrassed for grieving what has died. I know this is necessary to heal, and I ask for healing and comfort where growth means death in some way.

I want to continue walking into hope. Hope is life. I don't want to neglect what I'm leaving behind, but to celebrate that it was beautiful for a season. Please remind me where I need to grieve what's been outgrown and step forward into growth.

But grow in the grace and knowledge of our Lord and Savior Jesus Christ.
To him be the glory both now and to the day of eternity. Amen.
2 PETER 3:18 ESV

When I'm Tempted to Overextend Myself

Lord, I realize that sometimes I don't have to overextend myself. I can sit back and just be. There's so much comfort and grace in not having to be untrue to myself to be loved or not having to perform to get applause or to talk to be noticed.

I can cozy up and just listen. I can listen to You and to people around me. I can listen to Your Spirit in me. I confess that I notice how often I feel the need to overextend and give more than necessary. So, God, I ask for Your permission and Your gentle grace to guide me as I listen. I long to experience that deep knowing that occurs as I settle into how You tether my soul and weight me with grace. I can sit and just be and know that I'm okay. I'm okay. I'm okay. And perhaps being okay is the biggest grace today.

He says, "Be still, and know that I am God; I will be
exalted among the nations, I will be exalted in the earth."
Psalm 46:10 niv

A Forgiving Posture

It's hard to forgive when I'm in a defensive posture, when my heart is in a fight stance, when I'm ready to defend and argue and explain. I notice, God, that to live a life of forgiveness is to live a life open. You are the One who is speaking and advocating, and yet, when I settle back, when I ease into Your embrace, I can't simultaneously rest *and* fight. I can't simultaneously forgive *and* argue.

Where are the areas that I'm leaning forward in a fighting stance? Where is my heart hard? Where do I need to sit back and listen up? God, I'm asking You to make me aware of these postures today, and in their place, would You please forgive my defensive nature and soften me to take a posture of openness and emptiness and to be alert to You?

For anything that becomes visible is light. Therefore it says, "Awake,
O sleeper, and arise from the dead, and Christ will shine on you."
Ephesians 5:14 esv

128

Surrendering the Ideal

God, I confess I live for the ideal. The what-can-be. The best-case scenario. And with this longing for ideal, I find myself disappointed. Disappointed at what is. And disappointed at what could be. Because *all of life* can be so beautiful. Yet, You are making beauty even in the hard times. Even in the confusion and not-as-it-should-be, You are breaking through and saying, I Am.

Forgive me, Lord, for idolizing the ideal more than the reality of knowing You. Knowing You is enough because where You are is ideal. You are in the broken relationships and darkness. You are in the suffering and pain. You are in the not-just-yet. But deeper still is the beauty that You created me with a longing for more. And may this more be You. Kind, loving, omnipotent, mysterious *You*.

Lord, lift my face to see Yours and behold Your beauty. Your beauty beckons me onward and upward.

"Can you fathom the mysteries of God? Can you probe the limits of the Almighty? They are higher than the heavens above—what can you do? They are deeper than the depths below—what can you know? Their measure is longer than the earth and wider than the sea."
JOB 11:7–9 NIV

A Well-Stewarded Gift

You know what's funny, Lord? The very quality I was criticizing in someone is his greatest gift! I was focusing on his boundless energy and intense joy, but to have energy and use that passion to turn outward is a well-stewarded gift.

Lord, please forgive my criticalness. I admit, I'd rather have energy than sit idly and only move toward selfish desires. I want to use every ounce of energy I have to be a mirror of Your love and grace.

I ask You for the energy and stamina and soul joy to run passionately toward a selfless life—a life where I aim to serve, not be served. A life where I love before I'm loved. A life where I acknowledge that You are in all people and they are worthy to be respected and known. Thank You, Lord.

*Do everything readily and cheerfully—no bickering, no second-guessing allowed!
Go out into the world uncorrupted, a breath of fresh air in this squalid and
polluted society. Provide people with a glimpse of good living and of the living
God. Carry the light-giving Message into the night so I'll have good cause
to be proud of you on the day that Christ returns.*
PHILIPPIANS 2:14–16 MSG

Rest in the Rush

My soul feels rushed. There's no need to rush except for the deadline I put on myself. Why do I feel rushed?

Lord, I need Your calm today. I confess that I sense anxiety pulling at me, and more than ever, I need Your rest. Your deep, settled soul rest that anchors and pulls me back to Your throne room. This sanctuary space I often feel tempted to leave is exactly where You are calling. There's a tension here. A tension to stay with You and launch myself into the sea of rush. Deep breath in. Deep breath out.

Calm my mind, Lord. Still my soul. Weight me with Your love. Lord, please forgive me for living without margin and caving to a frantic pace. Oh, how I need Your rest today. Where Your rest is offered, help me find my way to You.

Then, because so many people were coming and going that they did not even have a chance to eat, he said to them, "Come with me by yourselves to a quiet place and get some rest."
MARK 6:31 NIV

Delighting in Differences

Differences can divide. Differences in politics and personalities and church preferences. Differences are where the enemy wreaks havoc and tears relationships, families, and churches apart.

Lord, where am I allowing differences to divide? Where am I focusing on what polarizes, instead of what connects and heals? Please lovingly convict me in this area and invite me to notice how You are bridging all of humanity to You. In my prayer, God, illuminate differences as an invitation to learn from others, to ask about their perspective, to be open to new ways of seeing and believing.

Where am I rigid and hard? Where am I judgmental and critical? Where am I pretentious and right? Soften me, Lord.

As I soften, may these different viewpoints melt into a kaleidoscope of humanity—unique ways Your Spirit moves through every race, language, doctrine, and opinion. Be my bridge, Father. Connect me to Your mercy and make me into a soft, moldable soul.

There is neither Jew nor Greek, there is neither slave nor free,
there is no male and female, for you are all one in Christ Jesus.
GALATIANS 3:28 ESV

Forgiving the Past

I find myself robotically sharing the ways I've messed up in the past, Lord. I'm quick to judge harshly and hold back grace for my faith journey. Yet, You don't see my past as a waste, but as necessary stepping-stones toward transformation.

When I look back at my past, where do I see You? Where were You when I fell short? When I lost my way? You were there. Offer me space to sit in this awareness even now.

When I kick into the well-worn path of "I really messed up," please bring to mind that even in my sin, You were with me. You see all and love me still. Show me how these dark moments were big-story invitations for Your grand plan.

How did these missteps lead me to the present? How did my struggle invite perspective? Compassion? Grace? Gratitude? Please shine a light on how You are using every experience to reflect Your grace to myself and others.

For as high as the heavens are above the earth, so great is his
steadfast love toward those who fear him; as far as the east is
from the west, so far does he remove our transgressions from us.
PSALM 103:11–12 ESV

More Manna

God, in the Old Testament, You offered manna to the Israelites. Enough for that day. Miraculous morning nourishment. God, I want Your manna as well. More of You. More everyday miracles and soul nourishment and daily reminders that You are providing and showing up and feeding my soul, mind, and body.

Where are You offering manna? Where are You providing and gifting and sending miracle reminders? Where am I neglecting to look down and find Your ground-covering gift? Lead me to Your manna, Lord. Let me nourish on Your truth. I long to fill myself with a content spirit and speak of the wondrous ways You cut through real time and provide.

Manna. Bring this word to my lips, and may I echo it throughout the day. *More manna.* More life. More miracles. More You. Thank You, Lord, for how You are providing.

"And he humbled you and let you hunger and fed you with manna, which you did not know, nor did your fathers know, that he might make you know that man does not live by bread alone, but man lives by every word that comes from the mouth of the LORD."
DEUTERONOMY 8:3 ESV

The Process

Do You know what's humorous, Lord? The actual word *forgiveness* means "the process of pardoning." It's a *process* to forgive. A two-steps-forward, one-step-back process. I assume that I'm supposed to forgive and be done. Honestly, though? I can't. I can't magically forgive and erase the painful moment or experience from my mind. I'm sorry for this. But I also take comfort that You know this forgiveness thing is a process. Some days will be easier, which is why I'm so grateful for Your grace.

Today is a harder day to forgive. I'm not there. So today would You please lavish Your grace on me? Remind me of the healthy steps I'm taking toward forgiveness, and may this be enough. Show me where there is a softening in my spirit, a move toward healing and repair.

Please saturate my thoughts in merciful reminders of how I am forgiving in light of how You forgive me. May Your Spirit remind me of and celebrate my process toward forgiveness one step at a time.

"Therefore do not worry about tomorrow, for tomorrow will worry about itself. Each day has enough trouble of its own."
MATTHEW 6:34 NIV

Awareness of Who or What to Forgive

Lord, as I seek Your strength to forgive, I admit I'm not sure what or who I ought to forgive. I ask for awareness. What are small, physical ways that my body hints at resentment or anger? Where do I bristle inside? Who do I find myself uncomfortable or frustrated with? Why? Where do I have trouble giving love and patience and an objective response?

I ask for Your awareness, Lord. For in paying attention, Your Spirit is shining tiny lights on where forgiveness is lacking. And how am I to forgive if I'm unaware of the sources?

In my prayer for awareness, please protect me, Jesus. Keep the enemy far from my ears and heart, and keep my tendency to blame at bay. May I walk into every moment with eyes open and my heart aware of what I am feeling, sensing, and thinking. I trust You to journey with me in my awareness and draw me toward healing and wholeness.

Examine yourselves, to see whether you are in the faith. Test yourselves.
Or do you not realize this about yourselves, that Jesus Christ
is in you?—unless indeed you fail to meet the test!
2 Corinthians 13:5 esv

Experiencing Jesus as My Brother

Jesus, I confess that I forget to experience You as Brother. I picture You far off, in the olden times, performing miracles with Your disciples.

As I read about how You suffered so that humanity can know You as a brother, I find myself crying. These tears are of disbelief, relief, and healing. For all I know is my earthly brother. If I'm honest, I simply want him to welcome my care and questions, to gently listen, and to be proud to call me his sister.

Jesus, how do You welcome me? How do we relate and connect? Are You proud that I am Your sister? May this new perspective and the truth that You are my Brother bring a renewed healing and quiet smile as I read, "I will tell of your name to my brothers; in the midst of the congregation I will sing your praise." Jesus, can we sing praises to our Father today?

For he who sanctifies and those who are sanctified all have one source. That is why he is not ashamed to call them brothers, saying, "I will tell of your name to my brothers; in the midst of the congregation I will sing your praise."
HEBREWS 2:11–12 ESV

137

Bitter Much?

God, don't laugh. You saw it. You saw me reach for the last bag of Halloween candy on the shelf and witnessed another woman swoop in like a bandit and steal the bag right from my hands!

The nerve! What will our sweet neighbor kids think when they come trick-or-treating and discover that we have no candy? Their Halloween will be ruined. They'll be in therapy for years. *Years.*

Jesus, I need You now. I need Your grace to lavish on this candy-stealing woman. Forgive her for her selfish ways. Is it okay if I pray that she gets ill, or that an army of high school children shows up at her door all night long?

Clearly, I have forgiveness and bitterness issues. Lord, thank You that I can laugh about this. Next year I will be better prepared.

Anyone who has been stealing must steal no longer, but
must work, doing something useful with their own hands,
that they may have something to share with those in need.
Ephesians 4:28 niv

When I'm Confused

God, sometimes I don't understand Your ways. You say "be still" in order to know that You are God, but the world tells me, "Work hard. Put yourself out there. Take action."

I feel the tension and wonder, *Which one is it? Do I stay still, or do I strive? Do I put myself out there?* I confess to You that I feel confused with this tension. I feel angry. I am frustrated with You asking me to sit and listen and notice and pay attention to where You are working, and yet simultaneously I wonder, *How will anything happen while I'm just "be"ing?*

So I bring this confusion to You and confess that I don't know what to do with it. Yet, I trust that You are doing a beautiful transformative work in asking me to "be." Perhaps this is the tension of trust? Belief that You are doing something even though I cannot see it? I trust You are doing something in the confusing, unseen pockets.

So do not throw away your confidence; it will be richly rewarded. You need to persevere so that when you have done the will of God, you will receive what he has promised.
HEBREWS 10:35–36 NIV

Community

God, I realize that I want to pick the friends that I think I need, and I confess that I don't always know what I need. Maybe what I need is what You desire for me. I'm acknowledging that I gravitate toward people with whom I'm like-minded.

Would You please surprise me? Would You pick my friends for me? Could I sense a connection, a stirring, and feel drawn to those who You want me to reach out to, listen to? God, my desire is to be able to bring out who You are in every person I meet.

You created me with a longing for deep connection—with You first, but with people as well. When it comes to community, would You please be the One who invites those friends? May I simply pay attention and say yes.

I appeal to you, brothers and sisters, in the name of our Lord Jesus Christ, that all of you agree with one another in what you say and that there be no divisions among you, but that you be perfectly united in mind and thought.
1 Corinthians 1:10 niv

A Musical, Out-of-the-Box Invitation

God, I get nervous before I sit down to play music. When I do, though, everything inside relaxes and feels at home and settled. You delight in music and tunes and songs. You weave notes and words and lyrics together. So much of music is echoed in Your creation.

God, could I learn to forgive even through songs? Are there songs that remind me of people I need to forgive? Are there songs that remind me of the ways I need to forgive myself?

Lord, please use music as an out-of-the-box invitation to notice where there are areas I need to surrender, release, and simply obey. Thank You for the gift of playing this musical instrument. I find playing awakens me from the inside out.

Praise the LORD. Praise God in his sanctuary; praise him in his mighty heavens. Praise him for his acts of power; praise him for his surpassing greatness. Praise him with the sounding of the trumpet, praise him with the harp and lyre, praise him with timbrel and dancing, praise him with the strings and pipe, praise him with the clash of cymbals, praise him with resounding cymbals.
PSALM 150:1–5 NIV

Taco Tuesday Prayer

God, our family started a fun tradition of making tacos every Tuesday and inviting whoever You put on our hearts, whether friends, a family, a single friend, or an older couple. I love that as we're sizzling meat, cutting tomatoes, stirring beans, and putting out chips and guacamole, Taco Tuesday becomes a celebration of small repetitions and traditions and people coming together to share a meal.

God, please turn my heart constantly toward the small—the small ways, the small ingredients, the small places that become a sacred space for connection and community. If this is the reason for Taco Tuesday, then may this be a conduit of the grace and space You offer to us through a meal and relationships.

Contribute to the needs of the saints
and seek to show hospitality.
Romans 12:13 esv

142

Teaching and Learning

I was just talking with a client, and she said powerful words that resonated: she goes into friendships to learn from people and to enjoy journeying with them, instead of feeling like she needs to come in as a mentor or offer wisdom. Please make me like her, Lord. Please make me a student. Forgive me where I've entered into a relationship thinking that I have something important to impart and neglecting to see us at eye level.

Help me teach, and as I do, please make me open to learning and seeing new perspectives, finding a new vantage point. Please broaden my viewpoints; bring people in my path from all ages, and put me in others' paths where I am constantly learning and curious. In growing, I long to learn from the most authentic Teacher—You.

For gaining wisdom and instruction; for understanding words of insight; for receiving instruction in prudent behavior, doing what is right and just and fair; for giving prudence to those who are simple, knowledge and discretion to the young— let the wise listen and add to their learning, and let the discerning get guidance.
PROVERBS 1:2–5 NIV

Follow Through

God, my brain is scattered. I can tell because I have clothes in various piles—on my chair, on the bed, on the floor. I haven't finished one thing well. I'm aware that this is a symptom of my scattered mind. I confess that I feel a bit topsy-turvy and in need of Your focused gaze.

Would You please look lovingly upon me? Would You please forgive me for where I attempt and don't follow through, where I start and don't finish? Would You give me grace to focus and have clarity and know where to put my time and attention in mind and heart?

As I focus, I want to hear Your voice. Would You please maximize those moments? Will You please celebrate when I accomplish one task at a time? I know that You meet me in the simplest ways, when I still myself and slow down and follow through.

Let your eyes look directly forward,
and your gaze be straight before you.
Proverbs 4:25 esv

Obedience

I want to do my own thing. I want to ignore Your voice and take the easy road. I want to join the comforts and safety of what society, and even our Christian culture, says. I want to veer off the trust path and ease into the coziness of security and circumstances and praying life goes easy. Even last night, when I prayed with our oldest child, his words convicted me: "God, help me have a good day." I realize so often I just want a good day. But what is a good day?

I want an uncomfortable day. *That* requires obedience. So today, Lord, I ask for strength. I thank You that You know that I'm going to be tempted to disobey; You intentionally speak about this in Your Word. In Deuteronomy 30, You say, "Obey and I will multiply your days."

Forgive my disobedience, and please pour out Your voice so that I can listen to it and from there, obey.

"Now if you obey me fully and keep my covenant, then out of all nations you will be my treasured possession. Although the whole earth is mine, you will be for me a kingdom of priests and a holy nation."
EXODUS 19:5–6 NIV

My Brokenness

Father, I neglect to face my lack, my brokenness, the ugly sin parts of my being. Yet, I can't ignore them when my ego surfaces in pride and judgment. Forgive me. Jesus, You took the heavy weight of the world and sacrificed Your life so I can taste salvation and sanctification through You. May I be mindful of this today. May I not move from this posture of repentance without feeling the gravity of my sin.

Thank You that You don't ask me to find my identity as a sinner, but as one who has eternal life through You. I ask for the depth of Your grace and forgiveness. May I feel this deep down in my bones. May I feel a portion of what You felt on the cross.

Shame. Pride. Envy. Lust. You saw it all and took it still. Thank You, my Savior, my Friend—my One who became sin so that I can spend eternity with You.

The LORD your God has blessed you in all the work of your hands. He has watched over your journey through this vast wilderness. These forty years the LORD your God has been with you, and you have not lacked anything.
DEUTERONOMY 2:7 NIV

Skywriter Signs

As I stare at the sky, I note one, two, *six* skywriters trailing a white line behind—like a spider weaving a web as it creates beauty. I laugh because, God, I know these skywriter lines are signs from You. Small reminders that You see me, that You know I'll be looking up and out to the horizon, searching for the subtle ways You speak.

You speak to me through skywriters' signs. They are there and seconds later vanish. An everyday miracle not recorded except in my mind. Yet I know. I tuck these sky lines inside and hold them close when I need a reminder that You speak not only in Your Word but also in personal ways.

Please forgive me when I forget Your sky gift. When it vanishes and with it, the memory of Your gift-wrapped miracle. Oh, how I ask for a million everyday miracles. Please pull my chin heavenward so I may look up and see—for a moment—Your skywriter signs.

He is the one you praise; he is your God, who performed for you those great and awesome wonders you saw with your own eyes.
DEUTERONOMY 10:21 NIV

When Shame Flares

Ugh. I note the flare of the familiar feeling of shame. Hot and heavy. And following shame hisses the voice, *You should be farther along. You shouldn't have to keep forgiving them.*

Lord, why is it I have to forgive this person over and over? Is something wrong with me, that I get triggered and angry and feel shame all over again? I confess I want to be done with this. I'm trying so hard to forgive, but the harder I try, the more shame I feel.

Jesus, would You please meet me in this shame? How do You see forgiveness? Where are You speaking to me about this process?

I know You long for me to live in freedom and forgiveness. Please teach me how to navigate the action of forgiveness without shaming myself for repetition.

Thank You for not keeping score. Thank You for knowing forgiveness is a process and that I'm doing the best I can. Shame is not welcome here.

He will again have compassion on us; he will tread our iniquities underfoot. You will cast all our sins into the depths of the sea.
MICAH 7:19 ESV

Parent Prayer

Lord, I'm aware of how hard I was on my parents. Where I saw lack and held it against them, forgive me. Where I saw celebration of performance and harbored anger, forgive me. Where I felt abandoned emotionally and put up walls, forgive me. Forgive me for seeing their pure attempts as half-empty.

As I parent my own children, Lord, please show me how to be sensitive to my kids' needs. Where do they need Your guidance? Your attention? Your truth? Your reminders? Your discipline? Please give me wisdom to parent them in such a way that they will know You intimately.

Where my children see my lack, please pour grace in the cracks. Where they hear impatient tones, pour in Your love. Where they see my brokenness, pour in mercy.

May my own parenting journey be one of gratitude and appreciation as I reflect on my own parents and affirm that they did the best they could, and a fine job at that.

No discipline seems pleasant at the time, but painful.
Later on, however, it produces a harvest of righteousness
and peace for those who have been trained by it.
Hebrews 12:11 niv

149

Appropriate Distance

I'm a sensitive soul, God. You know this about me. You created me this way. Yet, I confess how often I misinterpret my emotions to assume someone's response is pointed at me. This is not always the case. It's not about me. How someone responds is more about their process and circumstances and less about my personality. Forgive me where I've assumed. Forgive me where I've put up walls. Forgive me for where I've dimmed the sensitive parts of myself to be accepted and make people feel more comfortable.

Spirit, I trust You are working in all people. In all things. I surrender my need to insert myself in the middle of a relationship and feel responsible to care for it entirely. I ask for an appropriate distance, a holy objectivity, a wise knowing of when tension is about me and when it is about the other person. Give me clarity as I offer myself appropriate boundaries and distance and make room for my tender spirit.

I appeal to you, brothers, to watch out for those who
cause divisions and create obstacles contrary to the
doctrine that you have been taught; avoid them.
Romans 16:17 esv

What I Have Done for Christ

Much of my forgiveness journey is learning to forgive others because *I've* been forgiven. I come to You today, repentant for the daily ways I sin from my selfish desires.

Sin isn't something fun to sit in or think of. Yet, I'm asking You to bring to mind what my sins are. Where am I selfish? Where am I seeking validation? Where am I quick toward impatience and judgment?

I'm listening and noticing what comes to mind. As these sins surface, I'm asking for Your forgiveness. As I repent, I find myself less stuck in myself and more attuned to how You forgive so that I can offer forgiveness.

Jesus, what have I done for You? Where have I listened to You? Please talk to me about where I've selfishly pursued my own interests, as well as times I've put myself aside and turned toward You. Thank You, Jesus.

But the Lord said to Samuel, "Do not look on his appearance or on the height of his stature, because I have rejected him. For the Lord sees not as man sees: man looks on the outward appearance, but the Lord looks on the heart."
1 Samuel 16:7 ESV

Noticing What I Am Doing for Jesus

God, yesterday's prayer was about looking back on what I've done to meet You at the cross. Today, I'm asking, What am I doing for You in real time? Not because You need me to do things for You, but because the more I focus on You, the more I naturally align with Your awareness of my shortcomings and readily confess and move forward into truth in grace.

What am I doing for You today, Lord? What am I offering? What am I holding back? How am I reflecting You? Serving You? Worshipping You? Listening to You? Obeying You? Where am I resistant to do something for You because that would require surrendering my selfish desires?

In all these moments, Jesus, thank You for choosing me. I accept Your forgiveness and ask You to invite me to do life for You, in Your name. Amen.

But you are a chosen people, a royal priesthood, a holy nation,
God's special possession, that you may declare the praises of
him who called you out of darkness into his wonderful light.
1 Peter 2:9 niv

152

Noticing What I Ought to Do for Jesus

Where are You stirring and inviting me, Lord? As I think of Your self-sacrifice, bearing all sins, taking darkness upon Your body, dying so I can live, where are You asking me to live for You? What is it You created me to do in Your name? I realize my doing doesn't complete Your work but serves as a transformative testimony of Your forgiveness rooted in my obedience and action.

What ought I to do for You, Jesus? I'm listening. Where do I notice myself pulled and energized? Where do I feel obligated and tired? You are a Jesus of energy, not "shoulds." Anything churchy or legalistic or guilt-inducing is not what I ought to do for You. Instead, help me notice the "ought to" as an "I get to" invitation and confidently step into what You already began on the cross and will see to completion.

So Jesus said to the Jews who had believed him,
"If you abide in my word, you are truly my disciples."
JOHN 8:31 ESV

To Shine

Lord, why do I dim myself around certain people to be accepted or loved? This dimming is not from You. You created me to shine—not on my own to bring attention to myself but because Your glory is revealed through me. I ask for forgiveness for dimming, for shaming the deep, contemplative, big parts of me that I shrink small and quiet and closed off. Talk to me about why I do this. What would it look like to truly shine?

To live alive is to glorify You. How am I to forgive myself and others if I only offer the dimmed parts? Today I ask You to help me stand tall, to remove anything that threatens to dim and to move toward openness and vulnerability, to be a vessel of Your light.

"You are the light of the world. A city set on a hill cannot be hidden. Nor do people light a lamp and put it under a basket, but on a stand, and it gives light to all in the house. In the same way, let your light shine before others, so that they may see your good works and give glory to your Father who is in heaven."
MATTHEW 5:14–16 ESV

Confidence in the Unseen

God, I notice a pattern that I do well trusting when I see Your promises fulfilled, but when it's quiet or time goes by and there are no landmarks, I lose my footing and feel untethered and become scared. I doubt Your goodness.

I bring this to You, Jesus. I bring my doubt to You and ask for forgiveness. I wonder who else I do this with? When time goes by and I haven't connected with a friend, do I start to doubt our relationship? God, please forgive me when I'm so quick to forget, to lose confidence in You or a friendship when there's space or distance.

God, knowing this helps me be quick to forgive others when they are going through times when they need solidarity and my reaching out could be an encouragement to them. Please use my awareness of where I create distance and doubt to bring compassion and forgiveness to myself and others.

Now faith is the assurance of things hoped for,
the conviction of things not seen.
HEBREWS 11:1 ESV

Truth and Grace

As I lay down these plates and napkins and forks, as I put ice cubes into glasses and light candles, I see where You are nourishing with food but also with Your truth. Today I saw Your truth when I was confused about which decision to make, and right there, in John, You reminded me to follow truth and grace and to not do what everyone else is doing.

I so need these reminders as much as I need every meal, and these utensils to eat with and these plates to eat from. Lord, I need Your truth. I need Your grace. Thank You, even as I'm preparing to sit down to this meal. You are molding my heart into one that is hungry for truth and seeking You first. May I keep this at the forefront of my mind. Always.

For the law was given through Moses;
grace and truth came through Jesus Christ.
JOHN 1:17 ESV

Rain

It's drizzly and cold and raining outside. As I watch the drops fall, I think of how often You are watering and tending to the garden of our lives. God, where are the seeds You have planted? Where are the seeds I have planted? What does the ground look like?

Even as You send rain, You are watering what needs to sprout from the soil. I'm thankful for rain today—how it washes and clears and goes deep into the seeds that need to sprout. Rain is like forgiveness. Rain washes away all the extra and gets me to the heart of the matter.

What is in my heart? What is it growing? Is it blooming beauty? Weeds? May this blooming be a clear indication of what I'm planting and how Your watering is bringing things to life. May my life be a garden of beauty and forgiveness.

"Yet he has not left himself without testimony: He has shown kindness by giving you rain from heaven and crops in their seasons; he provides you with plenty of food and fills your hearts with joy."
ACTS 14:17 NIV

157

Resentful Feelings

I'm resentful today. I'm resentful of the love I've poured into people and not felt like it's come back. I'm resentful of the hard work I've invested and not seen the fruit of my labor. I'm resentful for trusting You and not seeing the next step. Jesus, I offer all my resentments to You.

I acknowledge these resentments and ask for Your forgiveness. This reminds me to ask You: Are there any resentments You have with me? Are there resentments people have with me? Are there ways people have poured into me that I haven't offered back, or said thank you, or been gracious or generous, or acknowledged their efforts?

Today, I surrender resentment. Thank You for forgiving the resentment I carry; would this not root into bitterness, but may this be a draw to live resentment-free and full of grace.

Love is patient and kind; love does not envy or boast;
it is not arrogant or rude. . . . Love bears all things,
believes all things, hopes all things, endures all things.
1 Corinthians 13:4–5, 7 esv

A Pasture Experience

God, when I read Psalm 23, I am drawn to the visual of a pasture. How I long to create that safe, soul-nourishing space. A place where I can come and be fully known and fully loved and find Your gentle care.

Where have You made me lie down to rest? Where are You walking beside still waters with me? What are those times in the darkest valley, and where have I noticed Your comfort?

God, I'm asking for Your provision as I make my home a pasture—a safe space where all who enter will come to know You and find truth and grace.

I know forgiveness is a part of traveling along the pasture. Thank You for meeting me there. Help me create a pasture experience wherever I am.

The LORD is my shepherd; I shall not want. He makes me lie down in green pastures. He leads me beside still waters. He restores my soul. He leads me in paths of righteousness for his name's sake.... Surely goodness and mercy shall follow me all the days of my life, and I shall dwell in the house of the LORD forever.
PSALM 23:1–3, 6 ESV

For the Interim

Jesus, You know I'm in a season of interim with moving and jobs and finding new community. I'm traversing what I left behind and still waiting for the pieces to come together in this new place. The in-between is scary and dim. I'm having trouble understanding why You stirred us to come here and how long I'll be in this middle space.

I confess, when puzzle pieces take a long time coming together, I start to look back and wonder if we made the wrong decision in moving and trusting Your call. I am scared, and having no confident answers for the future makes me feel wobbly inside.

Jesus, will You forgive my lack of faith in the interim? Will You please remind me of the moments You spoke? Will You bring those reminders now? Let me sit in these truths with You, so that when I feel wobbly, I can settle into this in-between and remember that You led me here and will not leave me.

"For I know the plans I have for you," declares the LORD, "plans to prosper you and not to harm you, plans to give you hope and a future."
JEREMIAH 29:11 NIV

Making a Birthday Cake

I'm pulling out ingredients to bake a birthday cake. As I crack eggs and stir, my mind wanders to birthdays when I wasn't celebrated, and suddenly I'm sad. I felt rejected and alone on those birthdays. How do I forgive those who forgot to celebrate my birthday, even as I'm creating a celebration cake for another?

Lord, help use this time to work it out, while I stir, whip frosting, and pour batter and think about all the things I love about the person I'm baking this cake for. Please join me as I process honest words about my own pain and channel forgotten birthday cakes by pouring all my love into this cake I'm baking for a friend.

And as I deliver this cake, may my friend feel celebrated and loved. I want her celebration to be an extension of a time I wasn't celebrated.

"Do to others as you would have them do to you."
LUKE 6:31 NIV

Soulful Conversation

God, I'm in need of some good deep, soulful conversation. I confess that small talk makes my soul wither. Deep connection, though? It feels like a big gulp of air. Deep, knowing air. For years I lived in the shallow end, forfeiting the deep waters for only small surfacy conversation, but now that I've tasted depth and authenticity, I crave these connections more and more.

God, in my desire for soul conversations, forgive me for dreading small talk. Help me realize that not everyone desires depth and emotions and vulnerability; help me to be okay meeting people where they are. In turn, I ask You to bring those who desire depth and spiritual conversations to my path, and to hold both in balance with Your Spirit.

Whoever walks with the wise becomes wise,
but the companion of fools will suffer harm.
PROVERBS 13:20 ESV

Root of Rants

Rants. They are everywhere. On social media. At family gatherings. Last night I found myself giving a ten-minute rant about nothing important. What's at the root of these rants? And how can I forgive those who feel the need to go on and on about trivial matters? Forgive me, Lord, for rolling my inner eyes when someone's rant begins, because in all honesty, this leads to my inner rant of judgment. What's my choice? Allow others to process and listen patiently? Shut off social media? Kindly excuse myself?

Why do we rant anyway? To be heard? To hear ourselves? To release all our thoughts in one long continual run-on sentence? Who knows. So today, God, I'm just asking for patience and grace when someone's rant begins. Perhaps all they need is for me to say, "I hear you."

The way of a fool is right in his own eyes, but a wise man listens to advice.
PROVERBS 12:15 ESV

The Grocery Line

It's almost dinnertime and I'm starving and the grocery line is long. Deep breath out. God, I admit, I just want to push everyone in front of me aside and put myself first. I have hungry mouths to feed. I have places to go. I clearly have a case of being impatient. Forgive me, Lord. Forgive me thinking often of, well, *me*.

How can I take advantage of this time as I wait in line? What can I notice? How can I find You here? Who can I ask a question of, or how can I pray for the person in front of me and the person behind me? What can I learn as I wait in this ridiculously long grocery line?

Grant me patience as I wait. Still me to go with the flow and be interruptible. Help me see You and the people around me, Lord.

Be completely humble and gentle; be patient,
bearing with one another in love.
EPHESIANS 4:2 NIV

The One Who Made You Late

I'm now late because of someone's failure to arrive on time. I feel angry and embarrassed. But I don't want to stay this way. I want to hear her reasoning, if she has one. If she doesn't, I want to forgive her, nonetheless. Because we're all human.

We're all late at some point, and the times I've been late I've desperately needed to be met with empathy and care and this gentle question: "Everything all right?" instead of a "Well, nice to see you finally made it." I don't need to heap shame on my friend.

Lord, please help me forgive the friend who made me late. Help me look from her perspective, ask clarifying questions, and really listen to what's happening below the surface.

Because the next time I'm tardy somewhere, I hope someone forgives me the same way.

"So whatever you wish that others would do to you,
do also to them, for this is the Law and the Prophets."
MATTHEW 7:12 ESV

Heaping Forgiveness

God, we're going to have a good long laugh about this one. Hear me out: I'm a bit perturbed at the neighbor who allowed her dog to poop in my front yard. On my newly mown lawn. By the newly planted flowers. Has she no concern? Did she not see what was happening? Does she think it's okay to leave a poop gift on my front lawn? I don't need to know. What I need is an extra dose of forgiving kindness to heap on her.

Because relationships matter more than holding grudges. She is my neighbor, and when You invite me to love my neighbor as myself, I believe You literally mean that. I'm asking for Your power to forgive, to turn this moment into a laughable experience so that when I see this neighbor, I can love her with true kindness that only comes from You.

"Their sins and lawless acts I will remember no more."
HEBREWS 10:17 NIV

Pause and Reflect

I am mad. Mama bear mad. A family member forgot to call my son on his birthday, my child who lives for affirmation and celebration, and my heart is broken for him. God, I need Your perspective right now. How can I advocate in a healthy way for my child, while not making this about me? How can I speak honestly without making this person feel bad?

Help me pause and reflect on what is true. Help me use this experience to note how my son feels loved and to communicate this to family ahead of time next year. Thank You for allowing me to see that my son feels loved in being remembered and called. Now, God, I ask for strength to forgive without holding resentment or a grudge. I ask for Your love to fill this pain and settle my anxiety. Help me use this protective mama love to lavish love on my child today.

"So watch yourselves. If your brother or sister sins against you, rebuke them; and if they repent, forgive them. Even if they sin against you seven times in a day and seven times come back to you saying, 'I repent,' you must forgive them."
LUKE 17:3–4 NIV

A Spiritual Invitation

Lord, what in the world? My neighbor called animal control on us when our dog wasn't even barking. How could he be so inconsiderate? Why didn't he come over to talk with us first? Why the passive-aggressive report instead of face-to-face words? I'm peeved. And confused. This is a neighbor I pass and wave to. We say hello when we take evening walks.

In my anger, God, please help me maintain sanity. I'm asking for Your power so that I don't sin. Or fly off the handle and say something I'll regret. I'm in need of a forgiving spirit and complete objectivity. Help this not be a personal matter, but a spiritual invitation. I'm not sure how, but please use this to teach me compassion for being around difficult people.

Therefore, as God's chosen people, holy and dearly loved, clothe yourselves with compassion, kindness, humility, gentleness and patience.
Colossians 3:12 NIV

A Burnt Meal

I did my best, Lord, but I burned the meal. Charred to a crisp. The whole house smells, and I feel embarrassed by this. I feel like I ought to be a better cook and manage my time and know exactly what this meal needed. I feel as if I let dinner down, as well as those I'm feeding. Was there ever a time, Jesus, when You burned dinner? When You went out fishing and charred those fish so that they weren't edible? I suppose You would've done a miracle and saved dinner.

Yet, I'm no miracle maker. I'm human. And when I forgive myself for being human and burning meals, I can have compassion on the other side. What is there for me to learn in this? Why do I feel like a failure for such an everyday mistake? If anything, this burnt meal signifies how life would be without Your redemption.

But if it is by grace, it is no longer on the basis of works;
otherwise grace would no longer be grace.
ROMANS 11:6 ESV

A Friend Who Forgot to Ask about Me

God, I'm noticing a pattern. I listen to this friend and ask how she is and leave the conversation without her asking how I am. Why does this bother me? Why am I feeling "off" in my spirit? Am I expecting too much? Giving too much? Carrying too much? I want to be a friend who listens and asks questions, and at the same time, I desire mutual interest.

Lord, please help me forgive this friend who forgets to ask about me. How can I love her without overlooking myself? How can I care without feeling hurt when we depart? I'm sitting in this awareness with You. What is it I need and expect, God? I'm asking for Your help to forgive her for her unawareness.

What is it You want me to do, Lord? May I listen and take this need into my next conversation with this friend and ask without needing to be asked. Help me have healthy expectations and boundaries in conversations moving forward.

"And when you stand praying, if you hold anything against anyone, forgive them, so that your Father in heaven may forgive you your sins."
MARK 11:25 NIV

A Prayer for a Late Bill

God, managing money is not my strong suit. I'm not defending my behavior but confessing this to You. Money is tight right now, and bills are late as a result. I feel such shame, such embarrassment, that I have to wait for money before paying this bill. Forgive me, Lord, for not managing my finances better.

You talk about the love of money being the root of all evil, but Lord, I feel like not having money also brings out evil in me. I'm so sorry for this. I need Your help.

Will You please provide? Would You bring financial opportunities? You see my needs and long to care for me. I ask in confidence, knowing the next bill I pay, I will give You praise for Your provision. I accept Your forgiveness for this late bill and hope it's the last.

"I will abundantly bless her provisions;
I will satisfy her poor with bread."
PSALM 132:15 ESV

The Drama Queen

God, let's have a frank conversation. You know drama queens? The ones who rush for the spotlight and direct all conversation to center on themselves? I admit, drama queens exhaust me, even though I'm sure I was one in my younger years. I want to run the opposite direction from them, yet You love them just as much as You love me.

I'm asking for Your wisdom and grace to forgive my drama queen friend. To know that underneath the showy behavior is a tender child longing to be seen, to be validated and celebrated and loved. Perhaps she especially needs to be loved when she isn't performing? Would You help me forgive and pay attention to why I'm annoyed? Would You transform my frustration into pure love for her? I wonder, who is she when there is no drama to speak of?

Please prepare my heart, Jesus, for our next interaction, and may it be honoring to You.

If you bite and devour each other, watch out or you
will be destroyed by each other. So I say, walk by the
Spirit, and you will not gratify the desires of the flesh.
GALATIANS 5:15–16 NIV

172

The One Who Refused to Apologize

I hurt someone's feelings and apologized and asked forgiveness. And she said nothing. No words. Nada. Zilch. Nothing.

How humbling this is. To sincerely ask for forgiveness and not be asked the same in return. Why am I hurt? What am I feeling inside? Do I think she owes me? I'm sitting with this bewilderment and know the root is pain. I want my pain to be seen and validated, and it's not.

I can't control her, Lord. I can't make her ask for my forgiveness or have a tender heart or want to see from my perspective. I can, however, ask for Your unconditional love to pour out of me and onto her; I can move forward into freedom without letting her weigh me down. I can forgive without strings, and perhaps this is what genuine confession is about: giving without receiving.

Each of you should give what you have decided in your heart to give,
not reluctantly or under compulsion, for God loves a cheerful giver.
2 Corinthians 9:7 niv

A Difficult Coworker

What is it about my coworker? I feel like he dismisses my ideas and rushes to one-up me. Constantly. I don't feel like my efforts are seen or appreciated. I feel like I'm making no difference or mark in the office, and I feel alone in this. Lord, I'm not sure why this coworker behaves dismissively, but I know in order to walk into work each day, I need to forgive.

I need to forgive, not necessarily for his sake, but for my health. Because if I don't, I foresee my health, my blood pressure, and my thoughts turning ugly. I want to be a light in this office, not a darkness. Jesus, please help me forgive my coworker. Help me smile. Help me bite my lip when I want to speak. Help me see through his behavior and into his heart. Help me know that this is not about me, but that I do have a choice in how I respond. Thank You.

Bearing with one another and, if one has a complaint against another, forgiving each other; as the Lord has forgiven you, so you also must forgive.
COLOSSIANS 3:13 ESV

Noticed and Affirmed

Lord, it seems the harder I work, the more I get silence from my boss. What is going on? Why does this seem so unbalanced? What am I hoping for? What do I need? If I'm honest, I know I feel unappreciated and unvalued. I hear nothing of the great strides, but only what I'm not doing to his expectations. I feel weary and borderline resentful.

Lord, help me forgive my boss who doesn't validate how hard I'm working. Please speak to me about the areas You are proud of me. Where do You see me working hard? How are You pleased? This is what matters most. Use this time to root me more confidently in who I am, even when I'm not noticed or affirmed. Help me forgive and move toward where my gifts are used and appreciated. Even if this is only from You.

For in Christ all the fullness of the Deity lives in bodily form, and in Christ you have been brought to fullness. He is the head over every power and authority.
COLOSSIANS 2:9–10 NIV

Reconstruction and Restoration

Lord, I'm pausing with thankfulness for the contractors working on our home. They are working so hard, and I can't help but wonder what their stories are. Where do they come from? What led them to this work? Do they have families?

Forgive me for focusing on the inconvenience of having a leak in our home and having mess and clutter everywhere. Point me to the reality that the need for construction pays the bills for these men. What appears as a minor setback and inconvenience in my week allows these contractors to use their gifts to fix and lay down floors and remodel home damage. Thank You for their gifts. Even as I hear them pounding and sawing and nailing, I am grateful for all parts of the body and how we work together for reconstruction and restoration.

For even when we were with you, we would give you this command:
If anyone is not willing to work, let him not eat. For we hear that
some among you walk in idleness, not busy at work, but busybodies.
Now such persons we command and encourage in the Lord Jesus
Christ to do their work quietly and to earn their own living.
2 Thessalonians 3:10–12 esv

Simplification

Oh Lord, come look at my closet with me. Do You see all these clothes? Yet, how often do You hear me complaining about not having anything to wear? I want more. The newest jeans. The cutest shoes. I love fashion and expressing myself through a fun wardrobe. Yet, I am aware of how much I waste. I have shirts I haven't worn in years.

Forgive me for having much and not taking advantage of these clothes. Please bring someone to mind, Lord, someone I can donate some of my clothes to so that she can enjoy and wear them, instead of them being wasted. Who would love this sweater? These shoes? These jeans?

Simplification is my prayer, Jesus. Simplification to use a few items and give away what I'm not wearing. As I simplify, turn my heart to focus on You and the gift of giving.

But godliness with contentment is great gain, for we brought
nothing into the world, and we cannot take anything out of the
world. But if we have food and clothing, with these we will be content.
1 Timothy 6:6–8 esv

177

The Critical Friend

Jesus, I have a critical friend. With her, life appears half-empty, full of sharp words, and followed by a negative aftertaste. I'm exhausted after time with this friend. In my exhaustion, I'm starting to judge her criticalness. The irony! Judgment for criticalness. Neither are life-giving. Forgive me for my judgment, please.

Please help me forgive her for her critical spirit. Where I try to show a positive side, where I rush to encourage, quiet my speech to listen. She is not a problem to be fixed. Nor do I need to spend lots of time in her presence if I walk away burdened instead of alive. Lord, help me reflect Your love and joy when I'm with her and not spend another ounce of energy stewing in her critical wake.

God, bring me to Your joy today.

"Judge not, that you be not judged. For with the judgment you pronounce you will be judged, and with the measure you use it will be measured to you."
MATTHEW 7:1–2 ESV

The Spouse Who Forgets

Okay, God, I don't understand. Does my spouse not hear me? Is he avoiding me? Is he just forgetful? Whatever the reason, I could use Your power to love and forgive him. Because I really just want to be mean and critical, and that's not helpful. In noticing his forgetfulness, turn me to see his heart.

What is he doing well? Where can I come alongside and celebrate the ways he does show up? How can I encourage instead of complain?

Lord, I need Your help to forgive. I long to speak honestly and with sincerity. Help me meet him where he is and prepare his heart to receive and take action. Regardless of how he responds, may I be quick to offer grace and believe the best in his intentions and actions.

Let all that you do be done in love.
1 Corinthians 16:14 esv

Honest Sharing

God, I need to forgive a friend who steals my ideas. I find myself afraid to share or speak honestly, for fear that my words quickly become hers. Why do I care? What's going on in my heart? Perhaps I'm feeling taken advantage of or a lack of trust.

God, I want to forgive this friend. I want to share honestly, without having to tuck my ideas safe and close. I want to trust that Your work is beyond bounds and that I don't need to live in scarcity but in plenty—including ideas. Help me know what is wise to share and what is best to keep quiet and hidden.

When I speak, may I give my words as a gift to be shared and reshared. When I look at my time with this friend as a ripple pattern of Your goodness, my attitude turns from stealing to multiplying. This is my prayer today.

Anyone who has been stealing must steal no longer, but must work,
doing something useful with their own hands, that they
may have something to share with those in need.
Ephesians 4:28 NIV

Jealousy

I'm ashamed to confess that I'm jealous of a friend's success. I'm envious and find myself comparing and falling short. And this grieves me, but I'm thankful I can be real with You and know You love me still.

Jesus, will You please forgive my jealousy? I want to celebrate my friend's gifts without minimizing mine. I want to illuminate her success without diminishing mine. I want to champion her voice without dimming mine. There's room for all of us to succeed, Lord.

For now, I see my friend's success, but draw my heart to know what is true: Your work is being done inside me. I feel the transformation. The slow deep sifting and surrendering. This isn't something to elevate or broadcast. This soul work is between the two of us. May this be my focus when I'm tempted to shift my eyes from Your face to her success.

But if you harbor bitter envy and selfish ambition in your hearts, do not boast about it or deny the truth. Such "wisdom" does not come down from heaven but is earthly, unspiritual, demonic. For where you have envy and selfish ambition, there you find disorder and every evil practice.
JAMES 3:14–16 NIV

181

Coping

Jesus, I know You made wine from water for a wedding celebration. I know You say it's okay to drink without getting drunk. Here is my honest confession: I drink wine out of habit and comfort, reaching for a glass to calm my busy mind. I can defend this behavior however I'd like, but my soul knows the truth: wine is a coping of sorts.

What does wine help me cope with? What does this habit create in my spirit? How do I imagine You as I enjoy wine? Are You pleased? Are You saddened?

There's a reason I'm aware of my wine indulgence, and I ask for You to forgive the parts that push past enjoyment and move into overindulgence. Talk to me about this, Jesus. I am listening and ready to respond.

And do not get drunk with wine, for that is debauchery, but be filled with the Spirit, addressing one another in psalms and hymns and spiritual songs, singing and making melody to the Lord with your heart, giving thanks always and for everything to God the Father in the name of our Lord Jesus Christ, submitting to one another out of reverence for Christ.
EPHESIANS 5:18–21 ESV

A Competitive Parent

There's a parent on my child's sport team who appears to be living out his younger sporty self. I'm annoyed and surprised by his competitive spirit. Lord, this is just a youth sport, an innocent game. I feel like it's turning into a push to win, compete, and be better than the rest. I don't like this atmosphere for my child or the other kids.

Lord, in noticing this competitive parent, help me offer a spirit of forgiveness and understanding. Perhaps this is how he connects with his child? Perhaps this is a way to pass time? A notch on his parenting belt? A bragging right? Whatever his reason, I don't have to understand, but simply love him.

What am I competitive about? It may not be sports, but work or my accomplishments. Help me not judge others before I'm ready to evaluate my own behavior. Help me reach for Your forgiveness and lavish love.

So that, as it is written, "Let the one who boasts, boast in the Lord."
1 Corinthians 1:31 esv

Concentrating at Church

I'm sitting here listening to our pastor and reading along in scripture and noticing the surrounding people—and, God, I confess I'm having a hard time focusing. I'm thinking about things at home that need to be done and work deadlines and relationships.

Please forgive me for being all over the place right now. Would You gently draw me back to sit with You and listen? May there be grace as I give my attention, as much as I can, to the words and songs, and as Your Spirit comes alive through scripture. At the same time, I'm thankful that I won't miss how Your Spirit is already moving. Your work on the cross does not depend on my focus. I get to participate and experience You as much as I offer myself and my attention.

So I'm offering what I can and asking that this be enough. Be my focus, Jesus. Thank You.

For those who live according to the flesh set their minds on the things of the flesh, but those who live according to the Spirit set their minds on the things of the Spirit.
ROMANS 8:5 ESV

184

Finishing What I Start

God, I get so excited and passionate and all-in, and then I lose energy to finish well. I lose the spark to follow through. I hate this about me. Why do I do this, God? What is at the root of my lack of follow-through? Do I feel like I need to do it perfectly? Do I feel like it doesn't really matter?

Would You please help me pay attention to why it is that I have trouble finishing some projects? What is this resistance in me? God, please forgive me for starting well and not finishing.

Today, would You please help me follow through and complete one task well? Would You help me sift through where to put my energy? Will You please walk along with me until I complete this? May I sense how You are noting what I do finish instead of shaming me for what's not yet done. You are a Father that sees the good and longs for me to be proud of my work, just as You are proud of me.

Better is the end of a thing than its beginning, and the
patient in spirit is better than the proud in spirit.
Ecclesiastes 7:8 esv

Celebrating Another's Accomplishments

God, I'm a selfish soul. I'm about what will bring me glory. My spirit is at war within itself. I want to praise You, and yet I want to be praised. Perhaps this is humanity. Nonetheless, it's icky. I ask for Your forgiveness in struggling to celebrate another friend's accomplishments. I find myself pausing and being jealous before I even have time to celebrate.

Lord, would You please clean out my selfishness and jealousy right now? Help me see the beauty this friend offers. You give each of us specific gifts, and they are to be celebrated. When we all work together and we all use our gifts, You are the One who is holy and glorified.

Today may I take a step and reach out to tell my friend that I'm proud of her. That I see her accomplishments and validate her hard work and see You glorified through her life. May this be an act of complete unselfishness done in Your name.

Rejoice with those who rejoice, weep with those who weep.
ROMANS 12:15 ESV

Housework

Isn't it funny, Lord, how much we've prayed for this home and now that we have it, I dread the housework? I don't want to clean the toilets. I don't want to dust. I don't want to remove the mold growing underneath our baseboards. Yet, this home is such a gift. Even as I vacuum floors, may I be thankful for what this home represents.

These dirty floors represent people who come in to be loved. These spills are a beautiful reminder of community and conversations and Your provision in this house. Every piece of dirt, every toilet that needs to be cleaned is a reminder that life is happening in our home. And life is where You live.

May I turn this housework into an act of worship. May I turn on music and relish in the hard work that is a result of Your answer to prayer for this home. I thank You for Your provision.

Whatever you do, work at it with all your heart, as working for the Lord, not for human masters, since you know that you will receive an inheritance from the Lord as a reward. It is the Lord Christ you are serving.
COLOSSIANS 3:23–24 NIV

An Active Faith

God, faith is a funny thing. Because faith lived with You is unpredictable and unknown. Active faith embodies mystery and awe and wonder; it is not calculated or comfortable. Yet, the enemy lies and tells us that if we're faithful, blessings abound, and I'm finding this not to be true.

When I look back in scripture and see Your faithful followers, those who lived an active faith, they suffered a ton. They laid down everything to follow You. God, I ask for Your forgiveness as I am often frustrated by what it looks like to live an active faith.

Active faith requires stepping into the uncomfortable, surrendering my ego. Active faith requires putting aside my desires to come alongside Your will. Lord, help me step into a life of active faith. Please forgive me for what I'm still holding on to. Please offer hope glimmers of what it looks like to take up Your cross and live a life of action, a life of faithfulness, a life of ongoing trust, even when it's scary and uncomfortable.

Now faith is the assurance of things hoped for,
the conviction of things not seen.
HEBREWS 11:1 ESV

Envying Others' Gifts

God, envy is my biggest hurdle. Envy of people's gifts. Envy of people being noticed. Envy of someone being elevated or spoken highly of. Envy of how another's gifts bring beauty. All this I confess to You. I'm not sure how to reconcile it. I'm not sure how to hold the gifts You've given me without looking at another and seeing what they are doing.

Forgive me, God, for this area that I continue to struggle with. What is it about this friend's gifts that I am envious of? Which of her giftings do I wish I had? As I sit with this awareness, God, will You please remind me of the gifts You've given me? They are unique and necessary. I want to live thankful for the gifts You've given instead of longing for another's, because then I'm wasting Your precious gift.

Please take this envy that churns and boils and replace it with confidence to do the work You've begun in me.

A tranquil heart gives life to the flesh,
but envy makes the bones rot.
Proverbs 14:30 esv

189

Wants

Jesus, I'm stilled by the first line in Psalm 23 about the Lord being my Shepherd, and me not wanting. Oh my goodness. *Want* is all I want.

I want a constant paycheck. More friends. Security. My husband to build trust bridges. My passions to come to fruition. See? I want, I want, I want.

I'm so clearly reminded that with You, I lack nothing. Lord, forgive me for all the areas I focus on want instead of focusing on what You've already given.

What are these areas? I'm going to be quiet and listen to You right now. Please show me how I'm not lacking. I lack nothing in these areas of want. May I settle into a quiet rhythm of noticing and putting those wants aside—not shaming them, not feeling guilty for wanting them, but simply noticing my wants. And then noticing that with You there is no lack. When I want those wants, may I gently put them aside and say, "Today I want You."

The Lord is my shepherd; I shall not want.
Psalm 23:1 esv

A Prayer for the Person Who Lied about Me

Lord, this prayer is loaded. A person lied about me. She smeared my name to people I look up to, who now look down on me. God, this hits me at the core because what I value most is truth and honesty, and this is not what is being shared about me.

My ego wants to defend and pull those people aside and say, "No, this is actually the truth." Yet, God, what would it look like to live trusting that You are fighting for me? That You are speaking on my behalf? There will always be people who choose to believe lies, and there will be those who long to seek truth. I'm asking that You bring truth seekers in my path. People who will believe the best, and if they don't, will clarify and ask to understand.

Please remind me not to believe what I hear but to investigate the truth—to go to the Source of all truth. I'm trusting that You will help me forgive the person who lied about me. You know the truth, and may I cling to that today.

The LORD detests lying lips, but he delights
in people who are trustworthy.
PROVERBS 12:22 NIV

191

Shepherding

God, my heart is broken at how Satan schemes to divide Your Church. He sneaks and attacks and whispers lies. He uses well-intended leadership to confuse the body. Lord, I need to forgive the pastor who did not shepherd our family. He led with people-pleasing and yeses instead of taking the narrow road.

This grieves my heart. This makes me so sad because You, as our Shepherd, care for each person. You saw the one wandering off, and You pursued that sheep, that person. God, when I notice those in church leadership who are not shepherding, when they are okay with people falling away, something in my spirit knows this is wrong. I need Your power to forgive them, because on my own I'm angry and look down on their leadership.

Soften me and use this to teach me to nurture and care, for we are all Your sheep; we are all Your people.

I pray for this pastor right now. Be with him. Be his Shepherd.

"Keep watch over yourselves and all the flock of which the Holy Spirit has made you overseers. Be shepherds of the church of God, which he bought with his own blood."
ACTS 20:28 NIV

Friends Who Stopped Friending

Lord, there was a friendship going along hunky-dory and suddenly our friendship stopped. She stopped reaching out and found other friends. I feel replaced and forgettable and sad and confused. I'm not sure what happened. When I asked her about it, she said, "Everything is fine."

Yet, our friendship feels off. It feels different. It lacks the intimacy it had before. Help me forgive her for not being the friend I want and need her to be. Help me to sit in this space of pain so I can really feel it and truly heal.

This may require spending less energy on those I feel obligated toward and instead focusing my energy on those friendships that are life-giving. My prayer is to forgive this friend. Let me hold this friendship open. I invite Your Spirit to come and do the healing. Thank You for being a constant companion, an unconditional friend. Thank You for being with me as I forgive this friend who isn't friending.

A man of many companions may come to ruin,
but there is a friend who sticks closer than a brother.
PROVERBS 18:24 ESV

For the Child Who Doesn't Listen

God, I find this a funny prayer to pray, because I need to forgive a child who isn't listening. I'm laughing because, was there ever a time that Jesus didn't listen to You? Or did He always listen? Maybe He's not a good example. Perhaps I look at Your other children, all of us humans who You are constantly parenting as we go about our merry way—totally disobedient and not listening.

In a way, this thought offers grace and compassion to forgive my own child who isn't listening, because I don't always listen. I don't heed every word. I don't stop at every invitation. I don't follow through with Your gentle guidance. I don't learn from Your discipline.

This gives me grace to forgive my child and also makes me laugh.

He replied, "Blessed rather are those who
hear the word of God and obey it."
Luke 11:28 niv

When I Was Grieving

God, forgive them, for they know not what they do. This is my prayer for the awkward comment said when I was in the throes of grief. Someone's words were unaware and hurtful, yet until one has experienced grief, it is awkward to approach this topic. Help me see her intent, instead of what she actually said. Help me speak lovingly and graciously about how her words made me feel and encourage her toward sensitivity and awareness. Help me not take her response to heart if she still doesn't understand and continues to offer awkward words.

Grief is awkward, Lord, and I'm thankful You know it firsthand and offer a safe space to be sad and to go to for comfort and healing. Where one person's awkward attempts sting, help me find solace in Your knowing embrace and permissive arms.

Jesus said, "Father, forgive them,
for they do not know what they are doing."
LUKE 23:34 NIV

The Lighting of a Candle

Such a beautiful, simple act in the lighting of a candle. As I do, I bring a forgiving, open heart to You and the people I interact with today. Strangers. Friends. Family. My kids. My spouse. My coworkers. All of these people are Your children, Lord. They are all seeking light in some way.

Before I head into my day of activities and work and pressing matters, may I be mindful of the light You offer as Your Spirit dwells in my soul. I hold the sacred reverence of this truth. Spirit indwelled—You take residence in my very being. You chose me as a vessel to shine in and from, reflecting Your glory to every person. May I get out of the way so that who they see is You. Your light. Your love. Your forgiving heart and desire for all of us to know You intimately and be changed by Your love.

In the lighting of this candle, I symbolically and literally agree to partake in union with You today.

"In the same way, let your light shine before others, that they may see your good deeds and glorify your Father in heaven."
MATTHEW 5:16 NIV

The Process of Aging

Lord, I notice age spots and gray hair and the skin around my knees showing age. Forgive me for the vanity that sets in as I long to cover these imperfections and hold on to my youth. As I think of how You created my body and what it has endured, I smile, for every wrinkle was earned in laughter or pain, every age spot carries a sun-soaked story of spending time in nature, playing and creating memories. The stretch marks reveal incredible people who I am honored to raise, and the gray hair hopefully reveals wisdom in my aging years.

Lord, may I grow older with grace. May my outward appearance reflect an inward confidence—a woman who knows pain and suffering and can courageously say, "It is well with my soul. I have Jesus. He is more than enough."

May every age reminder be a story illuminator, another year I've lived and loved and leaned closer into an intimate relationship with You. May each year encourage me to forgive quicker, listen deeper, and love stronger.

Therefore we do not lose heart. Though outwardly we are wasting away, yet inwardly we are being renewed day by day.
2 CORINTHIANS 4:16 NIV

A Teacher's Harsh Words

Jesus, my heart breaks for my child who experienced harsh words from a teacher. They were cold and critical and unnecessary. My mama bear anger wants to protect my child from pain, yet I'm coming to Your throne of grace to ask for insight to forgive this teacher. Forgive her for using harsh words to drive home a point. Forgive her for no doubt bringing her personal matters into the classroom. Forgive her for leaving a painful mark on undeserving ears.

Offer me strength to forgive this teacher—not only for what my heart will learn in this experience, but for how I can teach my child to forgive. Humans are a messy bunch. We hurt one another with and without intent.

I need Your grace and Your Holy Spirit–breathed words today, Lord, as I sift through how to talk with my child and model open communication with his teacher.

A soft answer turns away wrath, but a harsh word stirs up anger.
PROVERBS 15:1 ESV

Untapped Passion

Jesus, You know my prayer before it even leaves my lips. You created me with much passion and heart to come alongside how You are moving in and through me. I confess, I'm not sure what to do with this passion. I feel untapped, like a teakettle about to sing at the top of my lungs. I feel pent-up and about to burst.

What do I do with this untapped passion? How am I to use it? Where are You asking me to be still and wait? Where do You want me to take action? How do I glorify You through these passions?

Lord, in my lack of answers and uberpassionate soul, may I obediently take one step toward where You are moving. Just one step. And then another for the next day. May I find nourishment in Your daily bread and trust that You are revealing a reason for these gifts and that You will not let them go to waste.

Each of you should use whatever gift you have received to serve others,
as faithful stewards of God's grace in its various forms.
1 PETER 4:10 NIV

199

Abdicating My Ego

Perhaps the most painful part of forgiving, God, is abdicating my ego. Laying myself down. Surrendering my dreams and plans and significant accomplishments to rely wholly and fully on You. As I surrender my ego, I notice all the ugly and performance-based applause I crave. I see my striving and disingenuous following of the crowd. I feel my selfishness and the heavy weight of putting myself at the center. Forgive me for my ego, Lord.

Where I am quick to grasp at my ego and talk about myself, please quiet me. Where I am anxious to speak of my accomplishments to receive pats and accolades, please still me. Where I am quick to pad myself with a platform or numbers, please humble me.

I ask for peace. Quiet, still, deep knowing that Your peace is made perfect in my weakness. To surrender my ego makes room for Your strength, and this is where I want to live.

I know, O Lord, that the way of man is not in himself,
that it is not in man who walks to direct his steps.
JEREMIAH 10:23 ESV

Ethereal Embrace

Lord, I miss my dad. I miss his laugh and the way he heaved his shoulders. I miss the way he saw my kids and asked intentional questions. I miss his presence and humor and push to love others well. I miss everything about him. Sometimes I feel embarrassed for missing him when he's been gone for a while. As if I should be over it, as if grief has no business popping up years later. But this is a lie.

I know Your heart breaks for my broken heart. And even in missing my dad, I am thankful that I will get to see him in eternity.

Lord, please forgive me for the times I was impatient with my dad. For cross words and snarky stubbornness. I wish I could take these words back, but they echo in my memories. Forgive me, and in some way, would Your Spirit bring a peace reminder that as I ache for my earthly father, You offer comfort as my heavenly Father? I need Your comfort in a big, ethereal embrace.

You, Lord, hear the desire of the afflicted;
you encourage them, and you listen to their cry,
defending the fatherless and the oppressed.
Psalm 10:17–18 niv

The Friend Who Doesn't Know Christ

Jesus, I have a dear friend who doesn't yet know You. Help me not look at our time together as rushed or to be used to get her to arrive at Your doorstep. Instead, let us just be friends. Let us learn from each other. Help me trust that all truth is Your truth and that by being myself, Your Spirit is working and alive.

I draw on Your Spirit now. Forgive me for believing for a hot second that any of her salvation depends on our friendship. Please remove this holier-than-thou mind-set and replace it with the joy of journeying with her and inviting her to pay attention to Your work.

And one day when she comes to know You, may I be there to celebrate and remember all the ways You invited and stirred her to Your Spirit. Thank You for the mysterious ways You work.

*For by grace you have been saved through faith. And this is not your own
doing; it is the gift of God, not a result of works, so that no one may boast.
For we are his workmanship, created in Christ Jesus for good works,
which God prepared beforehand, that we should walk in them.*
EPHESIANS 2:8–10 ESV

202

A Bow on Every Challenge

Sweet Jesus, I need Your help to forgive my friend who wants to put a big fancy bow on every challenge that comes her way. "It's okay, God is good," she says. "It could be worse, I won't complain," she smiles.

And inside I'm screaming because I just want her to sit in the discomfort of challenges and feel the pain. To not feel like she must rush to a happy ending or put a bow on the situation. I find it hard to relate to her constant optimism and yet love her perspective.

I need Your forgiveness for where I am uncomfortable with her being comfortable. I also need to forgive her for not understanding what she doesn't understand—that You use our greatest pains to lavish Your deepest grace. We know You to be real only when we let ourselves become undone. And if she never goes to this place of feeling the sadness of a challenge, help me forgive her constant perkiness and pull from her contagious joy.

Lead me in your truth and teach me, for you are
the God of my salvation; for you I wait all the day long.
PSALM 25:5 ESV

I Am Alive!

Lord, this journey toward forgiveness is possible only because I am alive in You. You breathe life into my soul. You offer hope for the day ahead. You stir me toward repentance and confession and thankfulness. Time after time. Day after day. Every day is an invitation to live alive. To believe in Your love and let it root down to my bones and blossom high and beautiful so that others can partake in Your shade and beauty.

Today is another chance to forgive—to look inward and to surrender the parts that weigh me down in exchange for Your easy yoke. Thank You for journeying with me as I learn and relearn how to live alive and how to forgive myself and others.

Though I'll never forgive as fully as You did on the cross, for today, God, I am grateful to live alive—free of resentment, washed in Your blood, and basking in Your grace.

"Look, I am coming soon! My reward is with me, and I will give to each person according to what they have done. I am the Alpha and the Omega, the First and the Last, the Beginning and the End."
REVELATION 22:12–13 NIV

204

Anglican Prayer of Confession and Forgiveness

Most merciful God, we confess that we have sinned against You in thought, word, and deed, by what we have done, and by what we have left undone. We have not loved You with our whole heart; we have not loved our neighbors as ourselves. We are truly sorry and we humbly repent. For the sake of Your Son Jesus Christ, have mercy on us and forgive us; that we may delight in Your will, and walk in Your ways, to the glory of Your Name. Amen.

Scripture Index